ALISON
NOICE

3rd Edition

YACHTMASTER EXERCISES

FOR SAIL & POWER

Questions and Answers for the RYA
Yachtmaster® Certificates of Competence

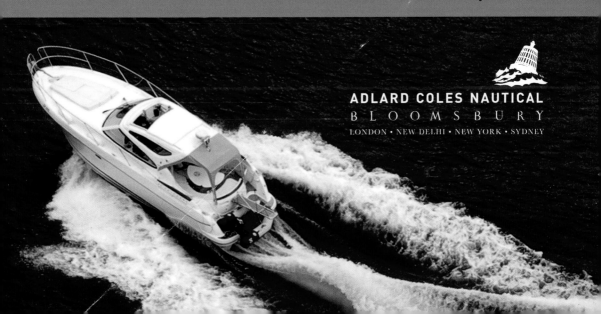

ADLARD COLES NAUTICAL
BLOOMSBURY
LONDON · NEW DELHI · NEW YORK · SYDNEY

Published by Adlard Coles Nautical
an imprint of Bloomsbury Publishing Plc
50 Bedford Square, London WC1B 3DP
www.adlardcoles.com

First edition 2005
Second edition 2010
Third edition 2012

ISBN: 978-1-4081-7810-2
E-pub: 978-1-4081-7814-0
E-PDF: 978-1-4081-7815-7

A CIP catalogue record for this book is available from the British Library.

Typeset in 9.25pt on 12pt The Sans Light
Printed and bound in India by Replika Press Pvt. Ltd.

Note: While all reasonable care has been taken in the production of this
publication, the publisher takes no responsibility for the use of the methods
or products described in the book.

**Yachtmaster is a trademark of the Royal Yachting Association registered
in the United Kingdom and selected marketing territories.**

Contents

Acknowledgements

My grateful thanks go to the following people who have helped with this book, and the companies who willingly gave permission for use of their material:

Adlard Coles Nautical	Reeds Nautical Almanac
International Maritime Organisation	Roger Seymour
Longbow Sail Training	Royal Yachting Association
Maritime & Coastguard Agency	Simrad
McMurdo	Stanford Maritime
Pains Wessex	UK Hydrographic Office
Raymarine	

Special thanks to Peter Noice, who took many photographs and constantly nursed my computer with never-ending patience.

Introduction

This book of exercises has been written to give student navigators the chance to perfect chartwork and seamanship skills learned from books such as Yachtmaster for Sail and Power or from RYA Navigation courses. The saying 'practice makes perfect' may sound trite, but it is infinitely preferable to get to grips with a subject in a warm, secure classroom than when the wind and sea are making life uncomfortable!

The subjects covered in the exercises are those in the RYA Coastal and Yachtmaster syllabus, and each exercise is graded with the more complex questions at the end. A Stanfords Channel Island chart has been included for the chartwork and passage planning exercises; this has proved ideal for the job as it gives a variety of places to visit, and rocky channels for pilotage problems.

The comprehensive step-by-step answer section explains how a solution has been achieved and should help establish an order of work when solving problems involving tidal height and course to steer. Emphasis has been placed on the use of modern electronic equipment without neglecting the vital traditional skills that need to be used in conjunction with them.

Finally, remember that all this theoretical knowledge needs to be put to good use where it matters most – out on the water. A few days spent navigating a boat on a coastal cruise is of more value than weeks spent in the classroom. There is nothing that surpasses the joyous feeling of entering a peaceful harbour after a tricky but safe passage with good friends as crew. After all, isn't that why you bought this book in the first place?

Alison Noice

Sunrise over Tortola

1 Charts

1.1

Is a straight line drawn on a Mercator chart:

(a) a rhumb line?   **b** a great circle?

1.2

Are the lines of latitude and longitude curved or straight on a Mercator chart? *Straight*

1.3

From where can you obtain corrections for Admiralty charts? *UKHO.gov.uk or boating Magazines*

1.4

How can electronic charts be updated? *electronically or exchange of cartridges*

1.5

What are the meanings of the following chart symbols?

a   **b**   **c**   **d**   **e**   **f**

1.6

In which Admiralty publication can the symbols above (and more) be found? *NP5011*

1.7

Charts can be based on a number of different datum. Which datum is used for the Stanfords chart enclosed with this book of exercises? *1950*

1.8

WGS 84 is the datum normally used by satellite navigation systems. What correction should be applied to WGS positions before it is plotted onto the Stanford's chart?

Safely moored.

Exercises ▪ 2

2 Compass

Use the Stanfords Channel Island chart to assist with answers to questions 2.1, 2.5, 2.10 and 2.11.

2.1

What is the magnetic variation to the west of Jersey in the year 2012?   3° 10' W

2.2

A compass can suffer from deviation. Explain the meaning of this statement. What are some of the possible causes of deviation?   Compass affected by magnetic materials in the boat, loud speakers, electric wiring etc.

2.3

Your autopilot is fitted with an electronic compass. Is this device subject to deviation?

2.4

You are at a boat jumble looking for a new steering compass for your fast sports boat. The vendor tells you that the one he is offering has been taken off a small yacht.

Will it be suitable for your boat? Give reasons.

2.5

You are in the vicinity of Plateau des Roches Douvres (left-hand side of the practice chart) and wish to fix your position using a handbearing compass.

Deviation &

Would a position so found be accurate or have a possible error? Give reasons.   Variation errors

2.6

What is the MAGNETIC bearing for each of the following?

a   034°T   Variation 12°W   022° M
b   001°T   Variation 3°E   004° M

2.7

What is the TRUE bearing for each of the following?

a   180°M   Variation 2°W   178°T
b   351°M   Variation 12°E   003° T

2.8

Use the deviation card (Fig 2.1) to calculate the TRUE course for each of the following. Variation is 3°W.

a   157°C 156°T c   000°C   356°T
b   215°C 212°T d   310°C   304°T

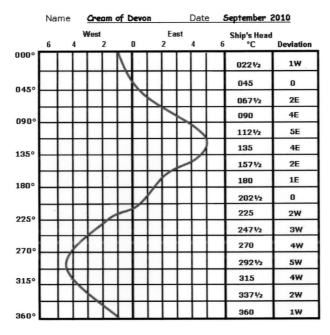

| Name | Cream of Devon | | | | | | | Date | September 2010 | |

FIG 2.1 Deviation card.

2.9

You are shaping a course to steer on the chart and will have to adjust for leeway in addition to variation and deviation before a compass course can be given to the helmsman.

In what order should the corrections be applied?   Variation   Deviation   leeway

2.10

A helmsman is approaching Guernsey from the southeast, keeping the Lower Heads South Cardinal Buoy in transit with the Al WR (alternating white and red) light on St Peter Port breakwater. The stream is slack and the magnetic variation is 3°W.

What is the deviation if the compass reading is 309°C? (Use the inset chart on the left-hand side of the practice chart).

2.11

In 2010, a boat is approaching Gorey (on the eastern side of Jersey) at slack water. The helmsman is using the leading lights in line to check the compass as he enters the harbour (see Fig 2.2).

If the compass reads 304°C, what is the deviation, if any? The variation is 3°W.

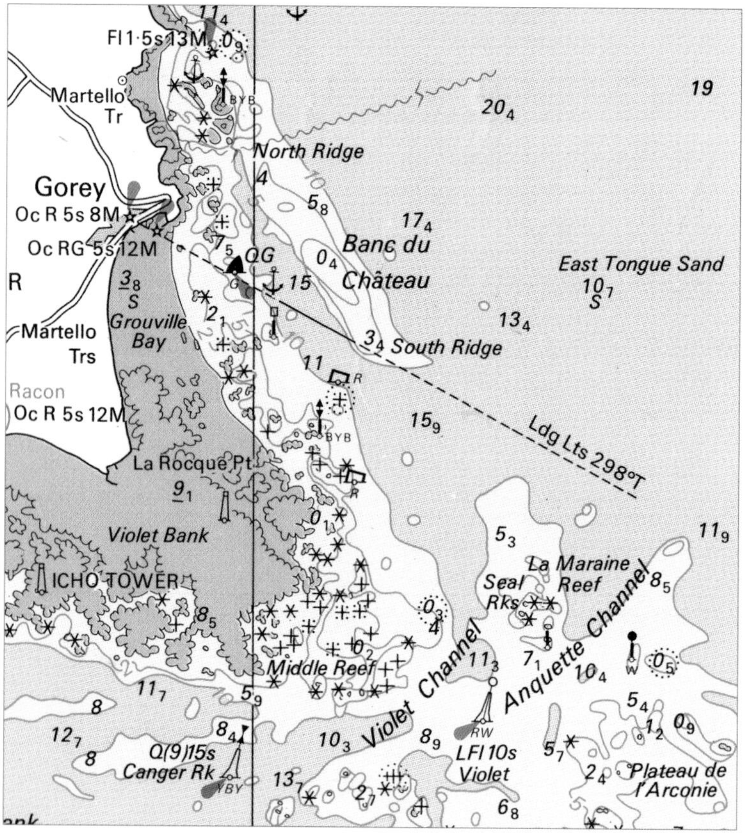

FIG **2.2** Leading lights for Gorey.

3 Position Fixing

Plot the fixes on the practice chart using 3°W variation.

3.1

At 0930, the following bearings were taken to the northeast of St Malo:

Monument on headland	209°M
Rochefort West Cardinal	260°M
Coastguard station	171°M

Plot the fix and give the latitude and longitude.   48° 43.2' N   01° 55° W

3.2

At 1030, the following bearings were taken.

Water tower at Cancale	241°M	01° 48.2' W
Signal station on headland	293°M	2.7 nm
Pierre de Herpin lighthouse	350°M	

Plot the fix and give the position as a bearing and distance from Cancale breakwater light.

3.3

At 0740, the following bearings were taken in moderate to poor visibility from a boat to the northeast of St Malo:

Rochefort West Cardinal	073°M
St Servantine Buoy	232°M

Comment on the reliability of this fix.

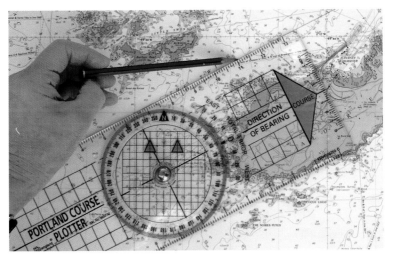

Marking a position line to plot a fix.

Exercises · 3

3.4

At 1430, when a boat on passage is near the southeast corner of Îles Chausey, the navigator notices that Le Pignon East Cardinal Mark is coming into transit with La Haute Foraine East Cardinal Mark. She takes a bearing on Les Huguenans isolated danger mark as they come into line. The bearing is 278°M.

Plot the fix. What is the depth below chart datum in that position?

3.5

The skipper of a boat on passage between Granville and St Malo has entered a special GPS waypoint at the centre of the compass rose closest to St Malo, to make position plotting less prone to error. At 1330, the position is given as 023°T 4.9M to the waypoint.

Plot this position and comment on how the position could be confirmed.

3.6

A boat with no GPS is on passage between St Malo and Granville on a night when the forecast is for fog banks. About halfway through the passage, the boat enters a fog bank but the skipper decides to continue towards Granville while keeping an accurate plot.

Later, at 0215, the fog clears in the local area and the depth sounder reads 14m (reduced to CD). At the same time, the following lights can be seen:

a   *To port*   An occulting white light with a 4 second sequence.
b   *Ahead*   A white light, very weak and difficult to see above the waves. One crew member thinks that it has nine flashes. It is difficult to take an accurate bearing of the buoy but it is thought to be within 5 degrees of 075°M.

Plot the boat's approximate position and draw the area of uncertainty.

Would it be safe to approach Granville if the fog comes down again?

4 Buoys, Lights and Lighthouses

4.1

What is the significance of the buoys in the photos below?

What is the colour and sequence of the light on each?

FIG **4.1** Buoys.

4.2

Using the Channel Islands chart, identify the type of buoy:

a in position 49° 41'.4N 01° 44'.5W.
b in position 308°T 1.9M from Le Grand Jardin lighthouse (north west of St Malo).

4.3

Explain the difference between a *flashing*, an *occulting* and an *isophase* light. Fl: darker periods longer
Oc: lit-up periods longer
Iso: equal periods of light darkness

4.4

a Which of the two posts in Fig 4.2 should be inserted at the division of the two channels if the one to the right were the preferred channel?
b What colour light would this post have?
c What would be the sequence of the light?

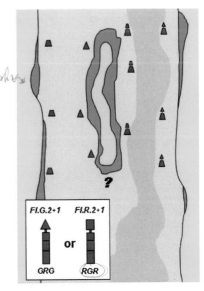

FIG **4.2** Channel buoyage.

Exercises • 4

4.5

The leading lights into St Malo from the northwest are described as FG.

What is the meaning of this abbreviation?   Fixed Green

4.6

Point Corbière lighthouse on the southwest corner of Jersey is shown as having the following characteristics: Some period between white & Red

Iso WR 10s 36m 18/16M Horn Mo (C) 60s

Describe *in full* what this means.

4.7

From a position 49° 18'.2N 002° 08'.6W to the north of Jersey, what would be the colour of the light at:

a   Sorel Point lighthouse? White
b   Grosnez Point lighthouse? Red

4.8

Use the rising and dipping table in Figure 4.3 to determine whether it is possible to see the light on Grand Léjon from the beach at Pléhérel Plage (on the mainland to the south east of the light)?

Lights – distance off when rising or dipping					
Height of Light			**Height of Eye**		
		metres	1	2	3
metres	feet	feet	3	7	10
10	33		8 7	9 5	10·2
12	39		9 3	10 1	10 8
14	46		9 9	10 7	11 4
16	53		10·4	11 2	11 9
18	59		10 9	11 7	12 4
20	66		11 4	12 2	12·9
22	72		11 9	12 7	13 4
24	79		12 3	13 1	13 8
26	85		12 7	13 5	14 2
28	92		13 1	13 9	14·6
30	98		13·5	14 3	15 0
32	105		13 9	14 7	15 4
34	112		14 2	15 0	15 7
36	118		14 6	15 4	16 1
38	125		14 9	15 7	16 4

FIG 4.3 Dipping Distance Table.

5 Tidal Heights

5.1

Which of the letters in the illustration (Fig 5.1) refer to the following?

i	Chart datum A	**v**	MLWN K	**ix**	H.A.T. M
ii	MHWS E	**vi**	Charted depth C	**x**	Charted height B
iii	Clearance height L	**vii**	Height of tide H	**xi**	MHWN G
iv	Depth of water J	**viii**	MLWS F	**xii**	Drying height D

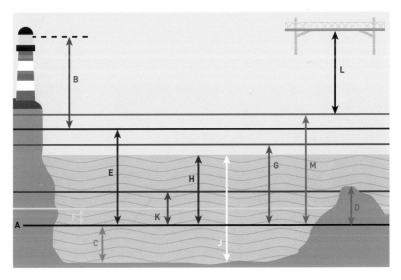

FIG 5.1 Tide levels.

5.2

The height of tide in Jersey (centre of chart) is calculated as 7.1m.   3.9∪

a   What is the depth of water 0.5M south of the inner leading light at Gorey?
b   What is the depth of water in position 49° 09'.1N 02° 12'.0W?

5.3

Use the tidal information given for St Helier (Fig 5.2) to answer the following:

a   What is the height of Point Corbière light above the
water at MLWN? 43 m
b   What depth of water will there be at MHWS over
the shallowest part of the Violet Bank (southeast of
Jersey)? 1.9 m
c   If a boat drawing 2.0m is anchored in the shallowest
part of St Aubin Bay (south Jersey) at MHWN, what
clearance will there be under the keel? 2.1 m

Standard Port ST HELIER				
Height (metres)				
HAT	MHWS	MHWN	MLWN	MLWS
12.2	11.0	8.1	4.0	1.4

FIG 5.2 St Helier levels.

d   What will be the clearance under a power cable with a clearance height of 14.0m at MLWS at St Helier?   24.8m

5.4

A bridge across a channel is shown as having a clearance height of 13m. The charted depth under the bridge is 0.8m and HAT is 5.7m.

What minimum height of tide will be needed for a boat drawing 1.5m and having an air draught of 15.0m to pass under the bridge with a minimum 1.0m clearance both under the boat and above the mast?   1.7m

5.5

What will be the height of tide at 2015 BST on Monday 25 October at St Helier?   7.30m

5.6

The skipper of a motor yacht with a draught of 1.2m wishes to cross a drying 1.5m patch off Cherbourg with a 1.0m clearance during the afternoon of Wednesday 10 November.

a   What height of tide is needed to give the required clearance?   3.7
b   At what time French Standard Time (FStanT) will the tide reach this level?   16°⁰

5.7

What is the minimum depth of water in which to anchor a boat with a draught of 1.8m to give a clearance of 1.0m at the next LW?

Date: Monday 13 September. *Place*: St Helier. *Time of anchoring*: 1000 BST.   6.5

Waiting for the tide at Emsworth.

5.8

What are the times and heights of HW and LW at Barfleur in the middle of the day on Saturday 23 October? Give the answer in French Summer Time (FSumT).

5.9

What are the times and heights of HW and LW at Braye (Alderney) in the middle of the day on Thursday 18 November? Give the answer in local time.

5.10

At 1130 FSumT on Wednesday 16 June, a yacht grounds just outside the entrance to Diélette, which is situated about 10M south of the Alderney Race on the west side of the Cherbourg peninsula.

a   What is the height of tide when she goes aground?
b   At what time will she re-float on the rising tide?

5.11

The skipper of a bilge keel yacht drawing 1.4m decides to dry the boat out in Barfleur to inspect possible damage to the propeller. He anchors in 3.0m of water at 1330 on Friday 1 October.

At what time (FSumT) will the boat:

a   Go aground?
b   Dry out completely?
c   Float off again later in the afternoon?

5.12

In what way could a low barometric pressure with storm force winds affect tidal heights in the vicinity of a depression?

5 20
600   -2.30
2.90 + 1 80 + 1.0   13

14   5.7

1.7m
0 8

6 Tidal Streams

Use the tidal diamond information given on the practice chart and the tidal stream charts at the back of the book. Times vary from question to question.

6.1

Use a course plotter and the tidal stream chartlets at the back of the book to find the direction and rate of the tidal stream:

a   Along the south coast of Guernsey, 6hrs after HW Dover at springs. 102° ~~1.1k~~ 2.4kn
b   Close to Portrieux, 2hrs before HW Dover at neaps. 335°   0.7kn
c   Five miles north of Cherbourg 4hrs before HW Dover, midway between neaps and springs. 90° 2.6

6.2

Use a course plotter and the tidal stream chartlets at the back of this book to find the direction and rate of the tidal stream:

a   Just north of St Malo between 0252 and 0352 BST on Tuesday 7 September.   1.4kn 260°
b   Close to the east of Guernsey between 0730 and 0830 BST on Saturday 16 October. 5.2kn 30°
c   On the northeast corner of Jersey between 1744 and 1844 UTC on Monday 1 November. 3kn 125°

6.3 ✓

Use tidal diamond ⓡ to find the direction and rate of the tidal stream:

a   3hrs after HW St Helier at springs. 283° 1.9 kn
b   At HW St Helier at neaps. 083° 0.3
c   2hrs before HW St Helier, midway between springs and neaps. 097° 1.6kn

FIG 6.1 Roustel Beacon, Guernsey.

6.4 ✓

Use tidal diamond Ⓐ to find the direction and rate of the tidal stream to the north of Cherbourg:

a   Between 0540 and 0640 BST on Sunday 17 October. 279° 1.1kn
b   Between 0914 and 1014 UTC on Thursday 4 November. 90° 1.6 kn
c   Between 1312 and 1412 BST on Monday 20 September.
     110° 0.95 kn

6.5

Using the tidal stream atlas, at what time during the morning (UTC) of Wednesday 24 November will the tide be slack between Jersey and Carteret?

6.6

On Friday 1 October it is intended to make passage between Cherbourg and Guernsey in a light displacement motor cruiser which is capable of 30kn. The weather forecast is for SW5 winds.

Between what times (BST) will the sea be most calm during the morning?

6.7

When planning a passage, what is meant by the phrase 'tidal gate'?

6.8

Are the following phrases TRUE or FALSE?

a   The stream is weakest in shallow water.
b   The range of the tide is never more than the mean range given in the Almanac.
c   The tidal stream can change direction at any time relative to local HW and LW.
d   The sea is roughest in a wind against tide situation.
e   The tidal stream runs strongly at neaps and is weaker at springs.
f   The stream around a prominent headland is usually stronger than along straight coast lines.

Exercises ▪ 7

7 Course to Steer

213 + 3   216°C

Use the practice chart and extracts at the back of the book. Use 3°W variation. Time zones vary from question to question.

7.1

At 1600, a boat is in position 49° 06'.8N 02° 09'.4W. The skipper intends to enter St Helier harbour (Jersey) and wishes to approach using the leading line. The boat speed is 5kn.

What is the magnetic course to steer to remain on the line while counteracting a tidal stream of 315°T 1.5kn?   *22k 042° M*

7.2

At 1115 BST, a motor cruiser is 1M due south of Point Corbière lighthouse (on the southwest corner of Jersey), wishing to go to the NW Minquiers buoy. The boat speed is 25kn and the tidal stream from 1100 to 1200 is 105°T 3.2kn.

a   What is the magnetic course to steer?
b   What is the approximate time that the cruiser will reach the buoy?

7.3

At 0800, a boat uses a GPS waypoint centred on the compass rose situated approximately 10M to the west of Jersey to plot the position that is given as 223°T 6.5M to the waypoint.

What is the magnetic course to steer to the Lower Heads South Cardinal Buoy (southeast of St Peter Port, Guernsey) with a boat speed of 6.5kn?

The tidal streams: 0800–0900 = 133°T 0.8kn
                            0900–1000 = 068°T 1.5kn

7.4

At 1340 BST on Sunday 17 October, a boat is in a position 1M due south of L'Etac rock on Sark, making for Désormes West Cardinal Mark, north of Jersey.

a   What is the time of HW St Helier? What is the range? Is it neaps or springs? *911 / 9.6 / Sp*
b   Using diamond ◇, what will be the tidal stream between 1340 and 1440? *242° 1.9 kts*
c   What is the magnetic course to steer to the buoy if the boat speed is 8kn?
d   At what time will the boat reach the buoy?

7.5

At 0215 UTC on Monday 8 November, a motor cruiser in position 49°27'.0N 02°26'.3W is heading for a point 0.5M due north of Bec du Nez lighthouse on Sark at a boat speed of 12kn.

a   What is the time of HW Dover? Is it neaps or springs?
b   Using the tidal stream charts and the rate to the southwest of the arrow, what will be the tidal stream at the time of the passage to Bec du Nez?
c   What will be the magnetic course to steer?

7.6

On Sunday 5 September, a yacht is sailing at 5kn well heeled on the starboard tack (wind blowing from the starboard side). At 1628, she is between Sark and Jersey in position 49° 18'.6N 02° 20'.0W.

a   Use the tidal stream charts to calculate the magnetic course to steer for a point 239°T from Grosnez Point lighthouse 2.8M.
b   If the yacht were making 10° leeway, what would be the magnetic course to steer?

7.7

A boat has NE Minquiers East Cardinal Mark entered into the GPS as a waypoint for plotting positions, and the position given on the display at 1130 BST on Friday 17 September is 139°M 2.0M to the buoy.

a   Using tidal diamond ◇N and the deviation curve in the extracts section, calculate the *compass* course to steer for the Mo(D)WR light outside St Helier if the boat speed is 7kn.
b   What will be the course over ground (COG) and the speed over ground (SOG)?
c   What will be the ETA at the light?

Evening calm in Kalkan, Turkey.

Exercises ▪ 8

8 Dead Reckoning and Estimated Position

Use the extracts section for tide tables, tidal stream charts, deviation card and harbour information. Use variation 3°W. Time zones vary from question to question.

8.1

Use the following information to plot the dead reckoning (DR) position at 1150:

1015	Close to Oc leading light at Erquy (approx 20M west of St Malo)
	Log reads 0.0M. Course 265°M
1100	Log reads 4.6M. Alters course to 225°M
1150	Log reads 9.9M. Drops anchor

Give the position as a true bearing and distance from the safe water mark in the area.

8.2

At 1230, a small boat is in position 0.6M due east of Caffa East Cardinal Mark heading 260°M at 4kn. The tidal stream has been estimated as 146°T 1.0kn.

a   Plot the estimated position (EP) at 1330 and give the latitude and longitude.
b   What is the COG (course over ground)?
c   What is the SOG (speed over ground)?

8.3

Fig 8.1 is an extract from the logbook of a motor cruiser on passage. Plot the EP at 1430 and express the position as a true bearing and distance to a waypoint at Men-Marc'h East Cardinal Beacon.

Time	Course	Log	Wind	L/Way	Baro	Depth	Notes
1400	000°M	1.9	S2	nil	1032	11.0m	0.4M west of Madeux Bn.
1430	000°M	14.0	S2	nil	1032	26.0m	Choppy water. EP plotted using tidal stream 160°T 2.4kn

FIG **8.1** Logbook extract.

8.4

At 1037 BST on Thursday 30 September, a yacht is in position 48° 41'.4N 02° 47'.8W, steering a course of 035°M. The distance log reads 3.2M at 1037.

a   What is the time of HW Dover? Is it springs or neaps?
b   Using the tidal stream charts, what is the direction and rate of the stream between 1037 and 1137?
c   Plot the EP at 1137 BST when the log reads 9.0M.
d   What is the COG and SOG?

8.5

At 0700, a yacht is in position 49°09'.8N 02°45'.8W, sailing close-hauled on a heading of 245°M, and the skipper is aiming to sail to the west of Plateau des Roches Douvres. Unfortunately, the neap stream is east-going so he decides to plot a projected EP to determine whether he will be clear of the danger area. He has calculated the tidal stream as 110°T 1.6kn and his average boat speed is 5½kn.

a   Plot the projected EP for 0800 and give the latitude and longitude.
b   Will the yacht be clear of the danger area?

8.6

Fig 8.2 is an extract from the logbook of a boat on passage from Saint-Quay-Portrieux to St Malo on Tuesday 23 November. Plot the EP at 1538 UTC.

Tuesday 23 November. Time Zone UTC.							
Time	Course	Log	Wind	L/Way	Baro	Depth	Notes
1338	060°M	6.7	W3	nil	1005	17.0m	Position:48°40'.0N 02°37'.6W
1425	060°M	11.0	W4	nil	1006	17.0m	A/C 095°M near Les Landas NCM
1538	095°M	18.6	W4	nil	1006	18.0m	EP plotted using ⟨Ⓡ⟩

FIG **8.2** Logbook extract.

Longbow II enjoying the strong wind.

Exercises ▪ 8

8.7

A yacht is on passage from Jersey to Saint-Quay-Portrieux and is approaching the Baie de St Brieuc. At 0953 BST on Thursday 14 October the position is fixed by GPS with reference to a waypoint centred on Grand Léjon lighthouse.

a If the position given at 0953 (log reading 31.3) is 245°T 3.9M, is the yacht to the east or to the west of Grand Léjon lighthouse?

b The yacht is logging 5kn on a heading of 185°C, making 5° leeway in a SE wind. What will be the direction of the line to be drawn on the chart?

c Using tidal diamond ◇, what will be the direction and rate of the tidal stream between 0953 and 1053?

d Will Petit Léjon beacon be to port or starboard as it is passed? How close will it be?

e If the boat speed and the tidal stream were to remain the same for the foreseeable future, would the yacht pass to the east of Caffa East Cardinal Beacon?

9 Instrumentation and GPS

9.1

The paddle wheel log is the type fitted to most small leisure craft.

a Give two possible reasons why the instrument could give inaccurate readings.

b Which would give you the most cause for concern – a log that is under-reading or one that is over-reading? Give reasons for your answer.

9.2

You charter a boat and find that it is fitted with a small radar set with an LCD screen.

a The charter company describes the set as 'unstabilised'. Does this mean that:

  1 The receiver is not gimballed?

  2 The radar picture will swing as the boat yaws from side to side?

  3 The antenna does not tip to compensate for the motion of the boat?

b What is meant by the phrase 'North Up'?

c A friend tells you that he always turns up the 'sea clutter' control until it clears all the white speckles off the screen. Is this advisable? Give reasons for your answer.

d What is the theoretical radar horizon for a boat with an antenna mounted 4m above the water?

e Will an antenna with a narrow beam width give better target discrimination than one with a wide beam width?

f Which of the following will be the better reflector of radar beams? The glassfibre hull of a large motorboat or the steel hull of a small boat?

FIG **9.1** Simrad Radar.

9.3

Your echo sounder gives unreliable readings in shallow water when the seabed is soft mud and also when passing through the wake of a big ship. Why is this?

9.4

How might you use your depth sounder to make certain that you are not dragging your anchor?

Exercises · 9

9.5

Is it best to have your GPS antenna mounted as high as possible on the mast or much lower down? Give reasons.

9.6

Are the following statements TRUE or FALSE? Give reasons for your answer.

a   State-of-the-art GPS sets use only three satellites for position fixing.
b   The GPS can be set to one of many different datums when in 'set-up' mode.
c   WGS 84 is the internationally recognised datum.
d   A GPS that uses 'Satellite Differential' will only be capable of giving a position to within 200m.

9.7

A crew member tells you that the HDoP reading on the GPS is high. What does this mean?

9.8

What is the meaning of the following abbreviations?

a XTE   b TTG   c SOG   d VMG

9.9

Dedicated chart plotters usually use vector charts, whereas those navigators using laptop computers as a chart plotter often use raster charts. Which of the following statements apply to vector charts?

a   The chart is simply an electronic scan of a conventional paper chart.
b   When zooming in, the amount of detail changes.
c   Data from the chart is grouped and stored in layers.
d   If the charts are over-magnified, the picture becomes blurred and individual pixels can be seen.

10 Pilotage

Use the extracts at the back of the book and inset charts on the practice chart where necessary. Use variation 3°W.

10.1

A boat is approaching Alderney from the southwest using the Swinge channel. The navigator is worried about hitting Corbet Rock and the off-lying rocks to the southwest of it.

a Use the chart of Alderney, in Figure 10.1 to suggest how major landmarks could be used to avoid the danger.

b How can the pilot check when it is safe to turn and head straight for the end of the breakwater?

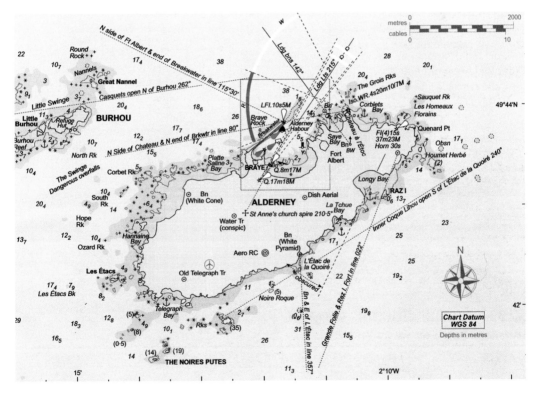

FIG 10.1 An extract from Stanfords Channel Island chart.

10.2

The skipper of a fast diving boat intends to return to Guernsey from Bouley Bay (north Jersey) after dark. The plan is to pass to the south of the Paternoster Rocks, and a waypoint at 49°16'.7N 02°14'.4W is entered into the portable GPS as part of the pilotage plan.

The boat gets underway and, once clear of the bay, the throttles are opened for a quick trip home. About 1½M short of the waypoint, one of the crew yells that he can see water breaking over a rock close to starboard.

a What is the likely position?
b What can have gone wrong with the plan?
c How could the skipper have avoided this mistake?

10.3

A boat is leaving St Malo at night using the leading lights viewed from astern to navigate safely in the channel (see inset on lower edge of chart). As Le Grand Jardin lighthouse is approached, the helmsman announces that he will have to alter course to port to avoid hitting the lighthouse!

Will the configuration of the lights look like illustration a) or b) in fig 10.2 when the boat is alongside the lighthouse?

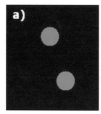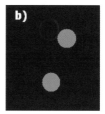

FIG 10.2 Which light configuration?

10.4

It is a perfect summer day in July with blue skies and a light breeze and ideal for a visit to Îles Chausey in a boat drawing 1.3m.

a A crew member suggests visiting the bird sanctuary – is this allowed?
b A boat arrives in Jersey from the UK then moves on to Îles Chausey. Is the skipper doing anything wrong?
c Which VHF channel does the harbourmaster use?
d Can you get a drink ashore on Chausey?
e What minimum height of tide would be required for an exit via the northwestern route if a 1.5m clearance under the keel is required?

10.5

A motor cruiser is preparing to enter the Bassin Vauban in St Malo. As the lock is approached, the skipper sees some lights on display (Fig 10.3).

What is the meaning of this signal? (See Extracts section at the back of the book.)

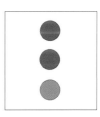

FIG **10.3** Lock lights.

10.6

A skipper planning to sail from Granville to St Malo on Sunday 20 June is preparing a pilotage plan and requires answers to the following questions:

a   Between which times during the morning (FSumT) is exit from the marina at Granville possible?
b   Why is care needed when leaving the marina?
c   Is it permitted to leave the marina under sail?
d   Where is the depth of water over the sill displayed?
e   The skipper decides to leave the marina as soon as the sill drops. What will the depth of water in the shallowest part of the entrance channel be at this time?
f   The yacht has a stiff sail to St Malo and arrives off Ile Harbour at 1330. Is it possible for the yacht to pass over the sill into Bas Sablons Marina at 1400 with a clearance of 1.0m or more under the keel?
g   On which VHF channel does the marina listen?
h   If the yacht got held up and missed the sill, is it possible to find anywhere to stop whilst waiting for the tide to rise again?

Exercises ∙ 11

11 Collision Regulations

11.1

How are the following defined in the IRPCS (Collision Regulations)?

a   A vessel not under command. *A vessel that cannot maneuver*
b   A sailing vessel. *Any vessel under sail, propelling machine not used*

11.2

When crossing a Traffic Separation Scheme, should the ground track or the heading be at right angles to the traffic flow? *Heading*

11.3

The illustrations in Fig 11.1 show situations where a risk of collision exists. Which is the 'give way' vessel and what action should the skipper take?

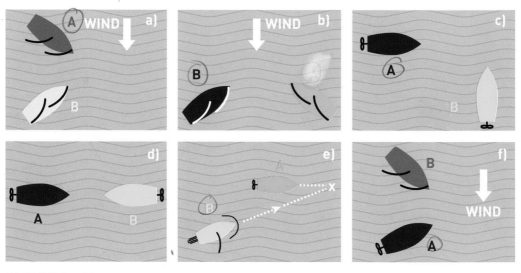

FIG **11.1** Collision risks.

11.4

Do the collision regulations give one vessel 'right of way'?

11.5

Can singlehanded sailors get special dispensation to ignore the 'look-out' rule when they are asleep?

11.6

Which two types of craft are specifically forbidden to impede other larger craft when in a narrow channel?

11.7

Draw a diagram of the flag which, according to the IRPCS, should be hoisted when there is a diver down and other vessels are required to keep clear.

11.8

What is the meaning of the day shapes shown in Fig 11.2?

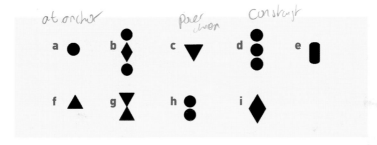

at anchor   power even   constrayt

FIG **11.2** Day shapes.

11.9

What are the meanings of the sound signals in Fig 11.3?

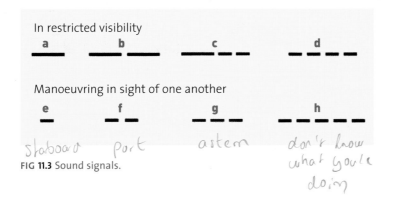

In restricted visibility

a   b   c   d

Manoeuvring in sight of one another

e   f   g   h

staboad   port   astern   don't know what you're doing

FIG **11.3** Sound signals.

Exercises ▪ 11

11.10

What type of vessel is shown in each of the illustrations in Fig 11.4? Mention its aspect, whether it is underway, making way, or has stopped, and what length is indicated.

MvC has stopped

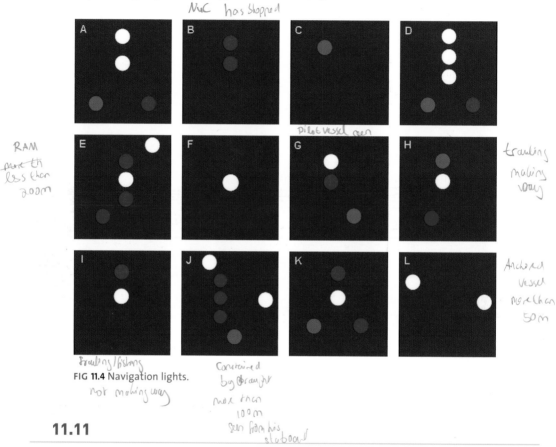

RAM
more th
less than
200m

Pilot vessel aen

trawling
making
way

Anchored
vessel
more than
50m

trawling / fishing
not moving way

FIG 11.4 Navigation lights.

Constrained
by draught
more than
100m
seen from his
staboard

11.11

What lights should be shown by:

a   a 10 metre yacht when motorsailing?
b   a 15 knot, 8 metre semi-rigid inflatable? *a white light*
c   a 6 knot, 6 metre semi-rigid inflatable?

12 Meteorology

12.1

What is the meaning of the following terms used in the shipping and other forecasts?

a   Slight
b   Moving steadily
c   Rough
d   Gale force

e   Imminent within 6hrs
f   Moderate
g   Cyclonic
h   Poor

i   Fair
j   Soon 6-12 hrs
k   Veering
l   Strong wind warning

12.2

a   Which way does the wind circulate around the area of high pressure shown in Fig 12.1? Is it clockwise or anticlockwise?
b   Would you expect the wind to be strong or light over the south of England?
c   Will this feature give unstable or stable conditions?
d   What will be the wind direction over NE Scotland?

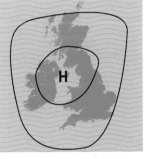

12.3

You are in the Irish Sea running north before a strong southerly wind. Is the area of low pressure to the east or to the west of you?

FIG **12.1** High pressure.

12.4

What Beaufort wind force fits the following open sea conditions?

a   Small waves, becoming longer; fairly frequent white horses.
b   Large waves begin to form; the white foam crests are more extensive. Probably some spray.

12.5

a   What type of cloud is shown in the photos below?
b   Would cloud A or cloud B be present ahead of a warm front?
c   Which cloud would give rise to showers and gusty conditions?

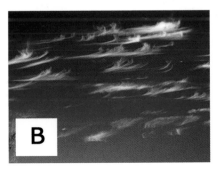

FIG **12.2** Cloud types.

12.6

For each of the illustrations in Fig 12.3, give the strength of wind (strong, moderate or light) and wind direction you would expect:

On the NE coast of England?   In the Dover Straits?   In the Bristol Channel?

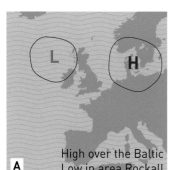

High over the Baltic
Low in area Rockall
A

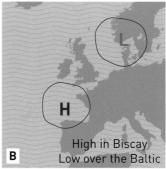

High in Biscay
Low over the Baltic
B

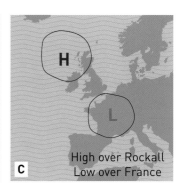

High over Rockall
Low over France
C

FIG **12.3** Diagrams for Q12.6.

12.7

Sea Fog
a   What conditions are necessary for the formation of sea (advection) fog?
b   At what time of year is it most prevalent in the English Channel?
c   What conditions are necessary for its dispersal?
d   Why does it frequently form around headlands?

Radiation Fog
e   At what times of the year does radiation fog form?
f   Will radiation burn off with the sun? Give reasons.

12.8

Use the weather chart in Fig 12.4 (opposite) to answer the following questions:

a   What will be the wind direction in Hebrides?
b   What weather feature lies in sea areas Hebrides and Bailey?
c   Will the barometric pressure be rising or falling in area Forties?
d   Will the visibility in sea area Plymouth be good or poor?
e   What type of cloud could you expect in sea area Dogger?
f   What type of conditions would you expect on the west coast of Ireland?

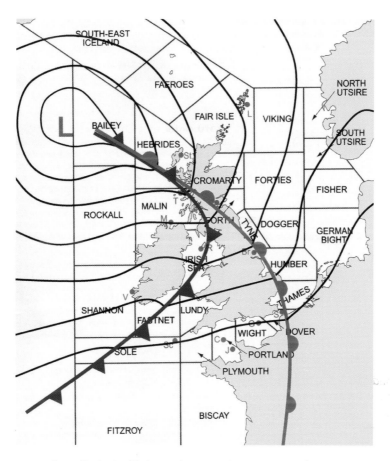

FIG **12.4** Synoptic chart with depression centred on sea area Bailey.

12.9

It is June and a large area of high pressure is centred over the UK. The forecast is for light and variable winds and sea breezes along the coast.

a Draw a diagram to show how the sea breeze forms.
b Will the wind tend to back or veer during the day?
c At what time of day will the breeze be strongest?
d What will conditions be like during the evening?

Exercises · 13

13 Safety and Communications

13.1

The motor cruiser *Sinking Feeling* has been holed after hitting an underwater object and is taking on water faster than it can be pumped out. After making sure that all three crew are safe, have donned lifejackets, and are preparing the liferaft for launch, the skipper then goes to the VHF DSC radio to send a distress alert and message. The position is given as 50° 10'.4N 001° 18'.6W (south of the Isle of Wight) The MMSI is 234002345 and the call sign is 2ZXY4.

a Describe the actions needed in order to send a DSC distress alert.

b What information is sent digitally when a DSC distress alert is made?

c Does the shore station acknowledge your alert:

    1 by voice only?   **2** digitally only?   **3** both digitally and by voice?

d Having sent the digital alert, how long should the skipper wait before sending the voice Mayday?

e Write down the voice distress message.

f Which has the greater range: a digital signal or the voice transmission?

FIG **13.1** Sinking Feeling.

13.2

A Search and Rescue helicopter is despatched to the stricken motor cruiser *Sinking Feeling*, which is now wallowing low in the water without any motive power.

a Does the HM Coastguard helicopter approach on the port or starboard side of the craft?

b What information is likely to be included in the briefing given on the VHF radio?

c What type of flare might the crew be asked to use to pinpoint the boat's position?

d Which type of flare should you definitely NOT use in close proximity of the helicopter?

13.3

Which VHF channel is:

FIG **13.2** Standard Horizon 1500 VHF DSC set.

a   the distress working and calling channel? 16
b   used as the primary inter-ship channel? 6, 8, 72, 77
c   used by HM Coastguard for small craft safety
     messages in the UK? 67
d   used to call the majority of marinas in the UK? 80

13.4

a   What type of information is given by the Coastguard during their regular Maritime Safety
     Information broadcasts?
b   Are these broadcasts made?
     ⓘ hourly   ii three hourly   iii four hourly

13.5

You are viewing a sailing yacht with a view to buying it, and the owner says that:

a   it has a high AVS. Explain what he means by this statement.
b   it is equipped with a 406MHz EPIRB. What is this and what would you have to do if you took
     over ownership of the vessel and the EPIRB?

13.6

A boat is equipped with an offshore flare pack. Which of
the three flares in the photo would be most suitable for:

a   signalling distress when 10M offshore?
b   daytime use in bright sunshine and light winds for pin-
     pointing the casualty's position in a distress situation?
c   pinpointing the position of a distressed craft within 3M
     of the shore?

FIG **13.3** Types of flare.

13.7

If you had just purchased a brand-new flare pack, how long would it be before you needed to
renew it?

13.8

You are entering an unfamiliar harbour at night. In the gloom you see that someone on a boat
in the harbour is using a torch to flash two white, short flashes and a long flash in your direction.

a   What does this mean?   b   What should you now do?

13.9

A boat is assisting the rescue services with a casualty at sea and has been communicating with
the searching aircraft. This aircraft overflies the boat and flashes his navigation lights twice. What
message is the aircraft giving to the boat?

Exercises ▪ 14

14 Planning and Making Passages

Use Stanfords Channel Island chart and 3°W variation. All times are given in BST and answers should be in BST. Use the extracts at the back of the book for port information.

Remember that International SOLAS rules legally require that a passage plan is made and that the following points (as a minimum) should be considered:

- *Weather*
- *Tidal height/stream*
- *Navigation hazards*
- *Crew ability*
- *Condition of vessel*

14.1

PASSAGE 1	
Date	Sunday 5 September.
Passage	St Helier to Diélette Marina.
Boat	A 12 metre twin screw motor yacht with a draught of 1.2m. It cruises at 25 knots in a smooth sea but at 8 knots when the seas are choppy.
Present position	St Helier Marina.
Jersey C/G forecast	Light south easterly at first with onshore sea breezes during the afternoon.
Crew	You as Skipper with your wife and two teenagers. All know the boat.

FIG 14.1 Passage from St Helier to Diélette Marina.

Use Fig 14.1 and the extracts to answer the following questions:

a What is the time of the morning HW at St Helier? Is it neaps, springs or mid range?   *1054 BST   mid-range*

b Between which times is there access to St Helier Marina? *0754 - 1354*

c Is there anywhere to wait in the port area if the marina is closed? *yes - waiting pontoon*

d You decide that the route around Corbière Point will be the less stressful route. What is the approximate distance and passage time to Diélette entrance? *15m 4· 40m   1h 30*

e At what time is HW Dover? *1558*

f Between which times is the tidal stream favourable for the passage? *1128 - 1228*

g Is access to Diélette outer harbour restricted in any way? *W*

h Use the tide difference on Dover (Diélette extracts) to determine between which times there is access to Diélette marina during the middle of the day. *828 - 1428*

i What dangers could be encountered en route?

j At what time will you leave St Helier? *1130*

k How can the skipper get information about wind strength outside the harbour? *Channel 18*

14.2

Now that the basic planning has been done, you decide to enter a route into the GPS using the following waypoints:

1	49°09'.6N	02°10'.0W	Approx 2 cables south of Noirmont Point	235°
2	49°10'.4N	02°17'.3W	Corbière lighthouse bears 073°T 1.6M	280°
3	49°14'.3N	02°18'.0W	Grosnez Point lighthouse bears 060°T 2.5M	353°
4	49°18'.5N	02°14'.2W	Depth 19.8m (reduced to datum)	32°T
5	49°33'.0N	01°54'.5W	0.5M NW of West Cardinal Mark off Cap Flammanville	41°T
6	49°33'.5N	01°52'.2W	0.5M NW of Diélette breakwater light	75°

Enter the waypoints on the chart. List the true bearings and distances between each.

14.3

At 1300, you are cruising at 24kn when you fix the boat's position with reference to the centre of the compass rose to the west of Diélette. The given position is: 345°T to the waypoint 5.1M. The log reads 86.1.

a   Plot the position at 1300 and give the latitude and longitude.
b   Using the tidal stream charts and the deviation card in the extracts section, what is the compass course to steer to waypoint 5?
c   At what time will you get to waypoint 5?

14.4

As you approach the harbour your propeller hits something in the water and appears to suffer some damage. Does the harbour have facilities for lifting boats?

14.5

PASSAGE 2	
Date	Wednesday 4 August.
Passage	St Peter Port, Guernsey to Granville on the Cherbourg Peninsula.
Boat	An 11 metre sailing yacht with 1.9m draught and an average cruising speed of 6 knots.
Present position	Victoria Marina at St Peter Port.
Shipping forecast 0048 BST	S or SE 4 or 5 veering W later and decreasing 3 or 4. Rain then at showers. Moderate becoming good.
Crew	Four in total – the Skipper is an experienced offshore sailor.

FIG **14.2** Passage from Guernsey to Granville.

Use Fig 14.2 and extract 13 to answer the questions below:

HW St Peter Port 0905 BST 9.2m.

a   Between which times during the morning could the yacht leave Victoria Marina with 0.5m under the keel?
b   Where may visitors berth in the outer harbour?

Exercises ▪ 14

Hard at chartwork.

14.6

a What is the approximate distance from St Peter Port entrance to the southwest corner of Jersey, and from there to Granville using the most direct route?

b Roughly how long will it take to reach southwest Jersey? And how long from there to Granville (excluding any tidal advantage)?

14.7

a Looking at the extracts for Granville, what is the time of HW at the relevant standard port during the evening of 4 August?

b What is the time difference between the standard port HW and HW Granville?

c Between which times during the evening is there access to Granville Marina?

d What is the time of HW Dover on the afternoon of 4 August? Is it neaps or springs?

e Looking at the tidal stream charts, what would be the best time to arrive at Granville during the evening?

14.8

a At what time would you exit the marina at St Peter Port?

b At what time would you leave St Peter Port for Granville?

14.9

Look back to the shipping forecast for 4 August (see Fig 14.2). What weather feature is due to pass over the area in the forecast period?

On passage

Use 3°W variation and the deviation card at the back of the book.

132+4
136°

14.10

126

The boat leaves the harbour at 1230 in the rain with moderate visibility and a fresh S wind. All the crew are looking forward to a bit of sunshine later on. The engine is switched off at 1300 when the Lower Heads Buoy is close to port. The skipper logs the position, zeros the log, and the boat sets off towards Jersey under reduced sail. It is estimated that, being well-heeled, the boat will make 10° leeway.

At 1400, in heavy rain and poor visibility, the skipper works up the estimated position to confirm the GPS fix. He records the information in Fig 14.3 in the logbook.

242° 1.9t

Time	Course	Log	Wind	L/Way	Baro	Depth	Notes
1300	135°C	0.0	S5	10°	1015	48m	At Lower Heads Buoy
1400	135°C	6.2	S5	10°	1014	50m	On S/B tack. EP using ⟨J⟩
							HW St Helier 0958BST Sp.
							GPS 49°22'.5N 02°22'.4W

FIG **14.3** Logbook extract.

a   Plot the estimated position at 1400 BST.
b   The GPS position differs from the one worked out for the EP. Give reasons why this may have happened.

14.11

At 1900 the boat is 2.0M due east of Les Ardentes East Cardinal Mark, logging 7kn in a moderate westerly wind. The log reads 41.4.

a   Calculate the compass course to steer to a point midway between Anvers East Cardinal Mark and Basse du Founet Beacon. Use the heavily printed arrow and accompanying rates when plotting this tidal stream. There is no leeway.
b   What is the SOG?

14.12

a   As the boat approaches Granville, the skipper checks his pilot book. What dangers are there in the vicinity of the port?
b   How can the skipper quickly check that his depth calculations are correct?

Chartwork test papers

15 Test Paper 1

Use variation 3°W. Use the extracts section at the back of the book where necessary. Time zones vary from question to question.

15.1

When just south of Alderney, a navigator takes the following bearings at 1010 UTC on Tuesday 2 November. The log reads 20.6.

Quénard Point Headland	006°M
Water tower	321°M
The Noire Putes (northern rock)	287°M

Plot the 1010 fix and give the latitude and longitude. ✓

15.2

From the 1010 UTC position, the navigator calculates the course to steer to a GPS waypoint off Cap de la Hague at 49°44'.4N 01°58'.4W using tidal diamond Ⓑ. 840T

a If the boat speed is 7kn, what answer does the navigator get?
b At what time (UTC) during the afternoon does the tidal stream become unfavourable around Cap de la Hague? 1341 UTC

15.3

The log extract in Fig 15.1 is from a yacht on passage from Alderney to Guernsey.

Plot the estimated positions at 0800 BST and at 0900 BST. 158°t

Thursday 21 October. Time Zone BST

Time	Co°C	Log	Wind	L/Way	Baro	Depth	Notes
0700	270	22.1	SW4/5	10°	1005	47.2m	Position:49°36'.2N 02°22'.0W
0800	270	26.6	SW4	10°	1004	53.6m	Tacked onto 170°C. EP using ◇
0900	170	30.7	SW3	10°	1004	10.1m	EP plotted using ◇

FIG 15.1 Logbook extract.

15.4

Tidal information for Barfleur is shown at the bottom of page 106.

At 1055 (FSumT) on Saturday 25 September, a yacht with a draught of 1.8m prepares to anchor off Barfleur.

a What are the heights and times (FSumT) of HW and LW in Barfleur during the day?
b What is the height of tide at 1055 FSumT?
c In what depth of water should the skipper anchor so that there is a 1.0m clearance at LW?

16 Test Paper 2

Use variation 3°W. Time zones vary from question to question. Use the extracts section at the back of the book where necessary.

16.1

At 1450 BST on Sunday 12 September, the following bearings were taken by the skipper of a motor cruiser off the north coast of Jersey. Plot the fix and give the latitude and longitude.

Western radio mast at Bouley Bay	161°M
TV mast	218°M
Sorel Point lighthouse	256°M

16.2

From the position of the 1450 BST fix, the skipper of the cruiser weighs anchor and steers a course of 023°C at 12kn en route for Diélette.

a Plot the estimated position at 1520 using tidal diamond .
b How far will the boat be from Les Dirouilles rocks at the closest point?
c At what time (BST) will the cruiser be closest to the rocky patch?
d What other method could the skipper have used to ensure that the boat remained at least 1M to the west of the rocks on Les Dirouilles?

Passage planning.

16.3

On Thursday 14 October, a yacht on passage from Diélette to Jersey is sailing on a fine reach in a SE wind. It is estimated that the yacht is making 5° leeway in a short choppy sea.

At 1420 BST, the navigator fixes position by GPS 222°T 3.6M using a waypoint at Plateau des Trois-Grunes West Cardinal Mark (north of Les Écrehou).

Use the tidal stream charts to determine the magnetic course to steer to a point 1.0M east of Écrevière South Cardinal Mark. The speed through the water is 4kn.

16.4

On Sunday 14 November, a skipper intends to dry his boat out in St Catherine's Bay on the east coast of Jersey in order to effect some underwater repairs. His boat draws 1.4m and he anchors in 3.0m of water at 0925UTC.

a   At what time (UTC) will the boat ground?
b   At what time (UTC) will the boat dry out?
c   At what time (UTC) will it re-float?

1 Charts

Steer 105 degrees, Skipper!

1.1

a A rhumb line – this line is not the shortest distance from A to B but as Mercator passage charts mostly cover a relatively small area compared with ocean crossing charts, the difference may be as little as a few hundred metres.

1.2

Lines of longitude and parallels of latitude are straight lines on Mercator charts, so forming a grid system for position fixing.

Answers ▪ 1

1.3

From the Notices to Mariners on the UK Hydrographic Office website (www.ukho.co.uk) and from some yachting magazines.

WALES

1303*	North Coast - Liverpool Bay - North Hoyle Wind Farm - Lights.
Insert	☆ 2Mo(U)15s14m10M, (F.R Lts) MAST(61) ....53° 25´·34N., 3° 28´·57W.
	Chart 1121 (INT 1062) [1157/04] Chart 1826 (INT 1607) [1302/04] Chart 1953 [452/04] Chart 1978 [452/04]
1542*	North Coast - Liverpool Bay - North Hoyle Wind Farm - Lights. Fog signals.
Amend	light at wind turbine to, (F.R Lts) Fl.Y.2·5s11m5M Horn
	Mo(U)30s ....53° 24´·45N., 3° 28´·17W.
	....53° 24´·79N., 3° 25´·33W.
	....53° 25´·72N., 3° 25´·64W.
	....53° 25´·38N., 3° 28´·47W.
	Chart 1953 [1303/04] Chart 1978 [1303/04]

FIG A1.1 Chart correction for Liverpool Bay from UKHO and *Practical Boat Owner*.

1.4

Chart cartridges can be taken into a main agent for electronic updating, or a disk of amendments may be supplied by some chartmakers.

1.5

a   Limit of restricted area.
b   Major light.
c   Yacht harbour, marina.
d   Rock which covers and uncovers with drying height.
e   Wreck, depth unknown, considered dangerous to surface navigation.
f   Rock, depth unknown, considered dangerous.

1.6

Admiralty Chart booklet 5011.

1.7

European datum 1950.

1.8

Positions should be moved 0.06 minutes NORTHWARD and 0.09 minutes EASTWARD to agree with the Stanford's chart.

2 Compass

2.1

It is fifteen years since 1997 and the variation decreases 7 mins annually. Subtract 105 mins from 4° 15' to find the answer of **2° 30'W**. For all practical purposes, 3°W would be used as the correction.

2.2

Deviation is an error that occurs when the boat's magnetic field affects the compass reading. Deviation can be caused by :

a   Ferrous objects such as the engine, iron keel, handheld flares and tool kits.
b   The electromagnetic effect from mobile phones, cables carrying electrical current and radio transmissions.
c   The magnetic influence from some large outboard motors, loudspeakers and analogue navigation instruments.

2.3

Yes, electronic (fluxgate) compasses suffer from deviation but, if set up correctly, are usually self-adjusting.

2.4

No, the yacht's compass will probably be insufficiently damped for your speedboat. The compass card may well behave erratically – or even spin.

FIG A2.1 Raymarine electronic compass.

2.5

The position could be inaccurate because magnetic anomalies are reported in the area (Fig A2.2). A GPS fix would be more accurate as magnetism is not used to fix the position.

FIG A2.2 Magnetic anomalies off the French coast.

2.6

a   034°T + 12°W = 046°M
b   001°T − 3°E = 358°M

Answers ▪ 2

2.7

a   180°M − 2°W   = 178°T
b   351°M + 12°E   = 003°T

2.8

a   157°C + 3°E   − 3°E   = 157°T
b   215°C − 0°   − 3°W = 212°T
c   000°C − 1°W − 3°W = 356°T
d   310°C − 4°W − 3°W = 303°T

2.9

1   Measure the angle of the TRUE course from the chart.
2   Correct for VARIATION.
3   Correct for LEEWAY.
4   Apply the appropriate correction for DEVIATION.

2.10

Transit = 308°T + 3°W Variation = 311°M.
Compass reads 309°C (compass least − error east) so the deviation is 3°E.

2.11

Leading line 298°T + 3°W Variation = 301°M.
Compass reads 304°C.
Deviation is therefore 3°W (Error west − compass best).

3 Position Fixing

3.1

See Plot (Fig A3.1). Fix at 0930 = 48° 43'.4N 001° 54'.9W.

3.2

See Plot (Fig A3.1). Position at 1030 = Cancale Breakwater light 043°T 2.7M.

3.3

See plot (Fig A3.1). This is an unreliable fix because only two objects have been used and the angle of cut is very narrow. Floating buoys are liable to shift position, particularly at LW, with such a large tidal range as the one experienced at St Malo. There has been no check on depth, but even if there had been, depths are often variable near the rocky plateaux off the coast and may not assist with pinpointing the position.

3.4

See plot (Fig A3.2). The fix lies very close to the 10m contour.

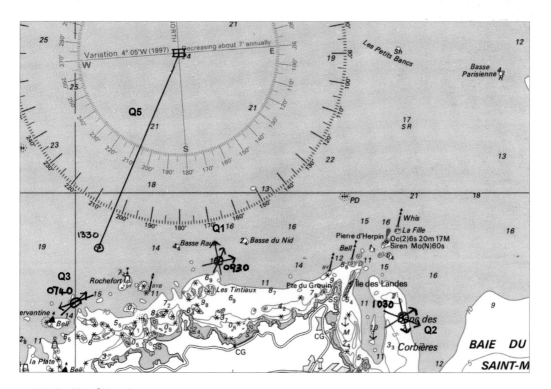

FIG **A3.1** Position fixing Q3.1, 3.2, 3.3, 3.5.

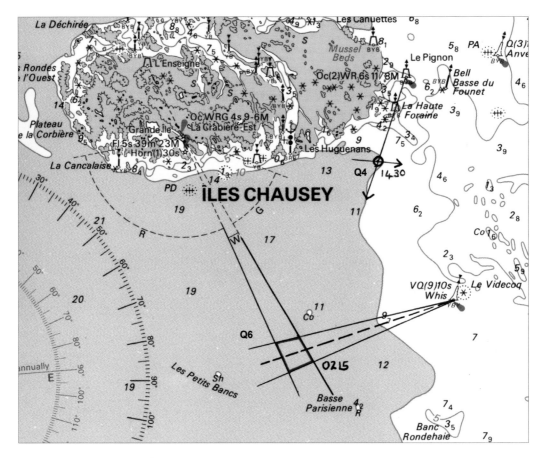

FIG **A3.2** Position Fixing Q3.4 & 3.6.

3.5

See plot (Fig A3.1). The depth sounder should read in the region of 16m, but this is not conclusive as the seabed is fairly flat over a large area to seaward of the rocks. Rochefort West Cardinal Beacon Tower should be clearly visible to port about a mile away and the East Cardinal Mark near the beacon should also be seen just to the left of the tower.

3.6

See Plot (Fig A3.2). The area of uncertainty is over half a square mile but is better than no fix at all. Provided that there is sufficient depth of water, it should be safe to proceed as the run into Granville is reasonably straightforward, although the depths are very varied. Point du Roc Lighthouse has a distinctive fog horn and a powerful light which should be seen through the mist at a safe distance. The fog may well thin over the shallower water as the coast is closed.

4 Buoys, Lights and Lighthouses

4.1

Photo **A** This cardinal mark is placed on the eastern side of a danger – keep to the east. The light is white, quick or very quick flashing in groups of three. The quick flash sequence takes 10 seconds and the very quick flashing, 5 seconds.

Photo **B** This buoy is placed near a newly reported wreck on a temporary basis. The light which flashes alternately yellow and blue is very distinctive.

Photo **C** An isolated danger mark which can be passed on either side. Horizontal bands of black, red, black with two black balls for a top mark. Light is white flashing in groups of 2.

4.2

a This cardinal mark is positioned to the north of a danger – pass to the north of the buoy.
Colour – Black over yellow.
Top mark – 2 x cones pointing upwards.
Light – White. Either quick or very quick flashing.

b A safe water mark or fairway buoy used to show that a line of lateral buoyage follows. It can be passed on either side.
Colour – red and white vertical stripes.
Top mark – one red ball.
Light – White, either occulting, isophase, long flash 10 seconds or Morse (A).

FIG **A4.1** North Cardinal Mark. FIG **A4.2** Safe Water Mark.

4.3

A *flashing* light is off for longer than it is on.
An *occulting* light is on for longer than it is off.
An *isophase* light has equal periods of light and dark.

4.4

a See Fig A4.3. The post which is predominantly red with a narrow green band as it is the port hand mark for the major channel and the starboard hand mark for the minor channel.

b A red light.

c Flashing 2 + 1.

4.5

The leading lights have a FIXED green light (ie they show a continuous light).

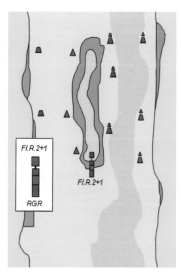

FIG **A4.3** Preferred Channel.

4.6

Point Corbière lighthouse has:

- An isophase light (equal periods of light and dark) with white and red sectors and a 10 second sequence.
- The centre of the light is 36m above MHWS.
- The nominal ranges of the white and red light are 18M and 16M respectively.
- The fog horn sounds with a letter C in Morse code, ie long, short, long, short, every 60 seconds.

4.7

a White. b Red.

4.8

No, it is not possible to see the light. The height of the light at Grand Léjon is 17m above MHWS and the height of eye would be approximately 2m when standing on the beach (see Fig A4.4). A dipping distance of just over 11M is found, and the distance to Pléhérel Plage is just over 13M.

Height of Light			Height of Eye			
		metres	1	2	3	4
metres	feet	feet	3	7	10	13
10	33		8·7	9·5	10·2	10·8
12	39		9·3	10·1	10·8	11·4
14	46		9·9	10·7	11·4	12·0
16	53		10·4	11·2	11·0	12·5
17m 18	59		10·9	11·7	12 **11.45nm**	
20	66		11·4	12·2	12·9	13·5
22	72		11·9	12·7	13·4	14·0

FIG **A4.4** Rising and Dipping Distances.

5 Tidal Heights

5.1

i	A	iii	L	v	K	vii	H	ix	M	xi	G
ii	E	iv	J	vi	C	viii	F	x	B	xii	D

5.2

a Height of tide = 7.1m less drying height of 3.8m. Depth of water is 3.3m.
b Charted depth 3.4m plus tide height 7.1m = depth of water of 10.5m.

5.3

a Difference between MHWS (11.0m) and MLWN (4.0m) = 7.0m.
Charted height of the light above MHWS = 36m.
Add difference of 7.0m to the height of the light = 43m.
b MHWS St Helier = 11.0m.
Violet Bank dries 9.1m.
Depth of water = 1.9m.
c St Aubin Bay dries 4.0m.
Height of MHWN = 8.1m.
Depth of water = 4.1m.
Boat draws 2.0m, therefore clearance = 2.1m.
d Height of MLWS = 1.4m.
Difference to HAT = 10.8m. Clearance under the cable is therefore 24.8m.

Starboard hand post with tide gauge.

5.4

Depth of water required = 1.5 draught + 1.0m clearance = 2.5m.
Charted depth = 0.8m so height of tide above datum required for 2.5m depth = 1.7m.
HAT = 5.7m
From 1.7m Ht of tide to HAT = 4.0m.
Clearance height of bridge = 13.0m above HAT
Clearance will be 17.0m when height of tide = 1.7m

Answer: 1.7m of tide will give at least 1.0m clearance between bridge and sea bed.

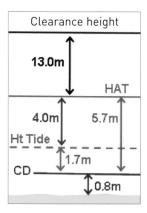

FIG **A5.1** Calculations for Q5.4.

5.5

Monday 25 October:

St Helier HW 1741 BST 10.2m. LW 1.8m. Range 8.4m (close to springs).
From tidal curve height of tide at 2015 = 7.3m.

5.6

Wednesday 10 November:

Cherbourg HW 1911 FStanT 6.0m. LW 1.8m. Range 4.2m (mid range and springs)

a   Height of tide required = 1.2m draught +1.0m clearance +1.5m drying height = 3.7m.
b   Time height of tide is 3.7m = 1600 FStanT (interpolating between the two curves).

5.7

Monday 13 September:

St Helier BST HW 0644 9.7m. LW 2.3m. Range 7.4m
From tidal curve: height of tide at 1000 = 6.0m above datum

Between 1000 and LW the tide will fall:	3.7m
Draught	1.8m
Clearance required	1.0m
Depth of water in which to anchor	6.5m

5.8

Saturday 23 October:

Cherbourg FStanT	LW	1140	2.6m	HW	1719	5.3m	
Differences		+0052	0.0m		+0105	+0.3m	
Barfleur FSumT		1332	2.6m		1924	5.6m	

5.9

Thursday 18 November:

St Helier (UTC)	HW	1017	9.4m	LW	1710	3.1m	
Braye differences		+0042	−4.0m		+0043	−1.2m	
Braye UTC		1059	5.4m		1753	1.9m	

5.10

Wednesday 16 June:

Range 7.5/7.9m, mid range.

St Malo FStanT	HW	0608	10.5m	LW	3.0m	HW 1823	10.9m
Diélette diffs		+0037	−2.1m		−0.5m	+0037	−2.2m
Diélette FSumT		0745	8.4m		2.5m	2000	8.7m

Boat grounds at 1130 which is HW +3hrs 45mins.
Height of tide at 1130 = 5.2m.

Enter time and height of next HW and recalculate when height of tide will be 5.2m on the rise. Remember to go halfway between the spring and neap curve.

Time height will reach 5.2m on rise = HW −2hrs 55mins = 1705 FSumT.

This porthand post should not be passed close to port!

5.11

Friday 1 October:

Cherbourg FStanT	HW 1023		6.3m	LW 1.3m	HW 2238	6.3m
Barfleur diffs	+0056		+0.1m	+0.0m	+0057	+0.1m
Barfleur FSumT	1219		6.4m	1.3m	(2nd) 0035	6.4m

From Cherbourg curve + Barfleur data: Height of tide = 6.0m (above datum).
Depth of water on anchoring = 3.0m, ie yacht is over a drying 3.0m patch.
Depth under the keel on anchoring = 1.6m.

Tide must therefore fall to 4.4m for grounding and to 3.0m to dry out completely.

a   Time of fall to 4.4m = +2hrs 45mins = 1504.
b   Time of fall to 3.0m = +4hrs 10mins = 1629.
c   Boat will float when height of tide = 4.4m at HW −2hrs 35mins at 2200.

5.12

Low barometric pressure in itself can produce tides that are higher than predicted. With no wind, the water would be 0.1m higher for every 11 millibars that the pressure is below 1,013 millibars. This means that with a barometer reading of 975 millibars (38 millibars lower than 1,013), the tide would be 0.35m higher than forecast.

This rise in height is further exacerbated when accompanied by strong winds, which raises the water level even more, causing flooding at HW. Tidal surges can happen when the wind pushes the water into a bay or estuary. The disastrous flooding in southeast England and Holland in 1953 was the result of such a tidal surge.

With very high pressure, problems occur when entering shallow harbours at LW springs. Great care needs to be taken to avoid a grounding and a long wait.

6 Tidal Streams

6.1

a   +6hrs Dover = 102°T2.4kn
b   −2hrs Dover = 330°T0.7kn
c   −4hrs Dover = approx 085°T 2.6kn (interpolating between 1.6kn and 3.6kn)

6.2

a   7 September:

HW Dover 0522 BST. Range 3.2m, neaps
HW hour 0452–0552
HW −2 0252–0352 260°T 1.4kn

b   16 October:

HW Dover 1301 BST. Range 6.0m, springs
HW hour 1231–1331
HW −5 0731–0831 BST. 035°T 5.2kn

c   1 November:

HW Dover 1314 UTC. Range 4.8m, mid range
HW hour 1244–1344
HW +5 1744–1844 130°T 3.0kn (by interpolation)

6.3

a   283°T1.9kn.
b   083°T0.3kn.
c   097°T1.65kn.

6.4

a   17 October:

HW St Helier 0911 BST. 11.0m. LW 1.4m. Range 9.6m, springs
HW hour = 0841–0941
HW −3 = 0541–0641 279°T 1.1kn

b   4 November:

HW St Helier 0944 UTC. 8.3m. LW 4.2m. Range 4.1m, neaps
HW hour 0914–1014 090°T 1.6kn

c   20 September:

HW St Helier 1042 BST. Range 7.1m, mid range
HW hour 1012–1112
HW +3 = 1312–1412 110°T 0.95kn

6.5

24 November:

HW Dover 0920 UTC
HW hour 0850–0950
Slack between Jersey and Carteret during the HW hour 0850–0950

6.6

1 October:

- Distance from Cherbourg to St Peter Port is approximately 40M, a passage of about 1½hrs (excluding tidal stream).
- HW Dover 1342 BST. Range 5.9m, springs. HW hour 1312–1412.

The sea will be calmest between HW –5 and HW –2 when the strongest stream is with the wind, and during the slack water period just after that. Even with the stream running strongly, the speed of the boat is sufficient to punch both the tidal stream and the wind. The passage can easily be completed between 0812 and 1112.

6.7

This is not a physical 'gate' in the true sense. It refers to the time when the tidal stream is favourable, ie the 'gate' is open. Cruising the Channel Islands successfully depends on getting the 'gate' times worked out as it is impossible to proceed against a spring stream of 7kn when your top speed is 6kn!

6.8

a   True. It is usually shallower inshore where the flow is slowed by surface friction.

b   False. At equinoctial springs the range can be far greater than the mean. For example, turn to the extract section and compare the range during the late evening of 29/30 September at St Helier with the mean range. The mean is 9.6m, but on that evening the actual range is 10.6m.

c   True. During the early afternoon of 30 September, HW Dover is at 1307 BST and it can be seen from the tidal stream atlas (extracts) that the stream turns from north-going to south-going off the eastern side of Guernsey at HW Dover –1½ at approx 1130. However, HW St Peter Port is at 0831 BST, which means that the stream outside St Peter Port entrance changes at local HW +3.

d   True. The Alderney Race has streams of up to 10kn at springs, and when this stream has strong winds blowing against it, the area becomes a maelstrom – not a pretty sight!

e   False.

f   True. Any prominent headland will cause the water to deviate around it. As the stream bends, it accelerates – as shown in the illustration of the notorious Portland Race (Fig A6.1).

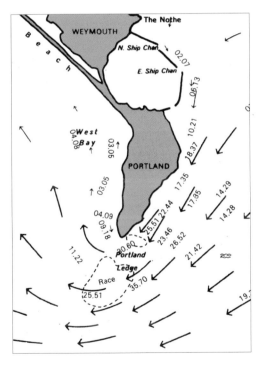

FIG A6.1 Portland tidal streams.

Answers · 7

7 Course to Steer

7.1

See Fig A7.1.

CTS = 039°T + 3°W = 042°M.

7.2

See Fig A7.2.

a CTS = 207°T + 3°W = 210°M.
b Approx 25mins run. The cruiser will reach the buoy at approximately 1140 BST.

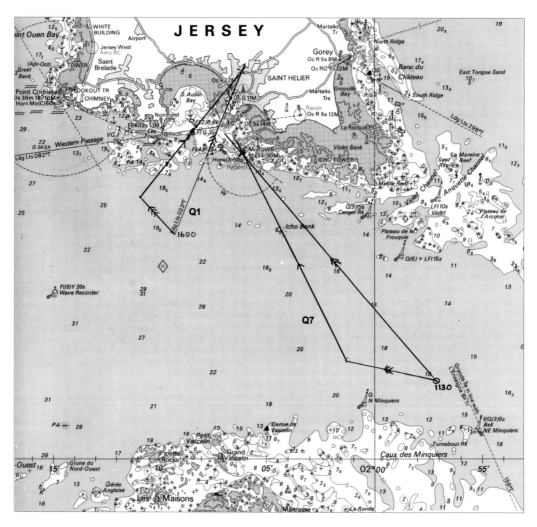

FIG **A7.1** Course to Steer Q7.1 & 7.7.

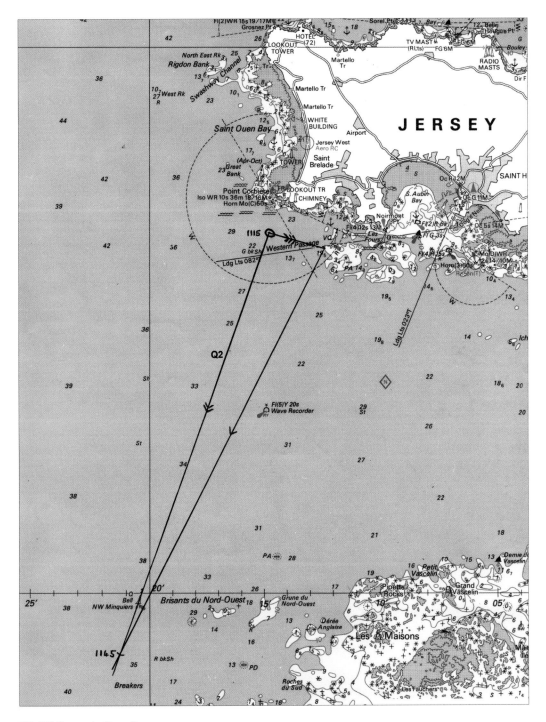

FIG A7.2 Course to Steer Q7.2.

7.3

See Fig A7.3.

CTS = $344°T + 3°W = 347°M$.

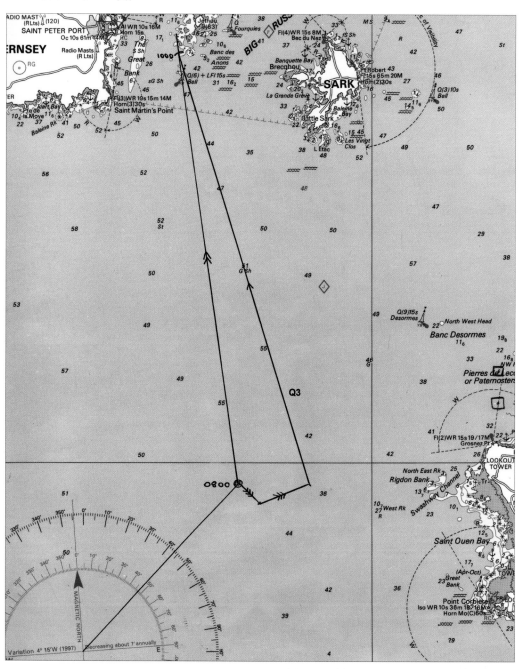

FIG A7.3 Course to Steer Q7.3.

7.4

See Fig A7.4.

17 October:

a   HW St Helier 0911 BST. Range 9.5m, springs.
b   HW hour = 0841–0941.
     HW +5hrs 1341–1441 242°T 1.8kn.
c   CTS = 134°T + 3°W = 137°M.
d   Distance to the buoy (4.9M) ÷ speed over ground (7.6kn) x 60 = 39mins.
     Boat will reach the buoy at 1340 + 39 mins = 1419 BST.

7.5

See Fig A7.5.

8 November:

a   HW Dover 0736 UTC. Range 3.2m, neaps.
b   HW hour 0706–0806.
     Period of passage HW −5hrs 0206–0306 = 037°T 2.5kn.
c   Passage will take about 15mins, but draw a plot for ½hr.
     CTS = 085°T + 3°W = 088°M.

7.6

See Fig A7.4.

5 September:

a   HW Dover 1558 BST. Range 4.5m, mid range.
     HW hour 1528–1628.
     HW +1hr 1628–1728 239°T. Spring 2.4kn. Neap 1.0kn. Mid 1.7kn.
     CTS = 148°T + 3°W = 151°M.
b   To correct for 10° push to port, it will be necessary to alter 10° to starboard (into the wind to stay on track.
     CTS with leeway = 151°M + 10° = 161°M.

7.7

See Fig A7.1.

17 September:

a   HW St Helier 0901 BST. Range 9.7m, springs.
     HW hour = 0831–0931.
     Time of passage = HW +3hrs = 1131–1231.
     ◇ 282°T 2.9kn.
     CTS = 333°T + Variation 3°W = 336°M + Deviation 3°W = 339°C.
b   COG = 319°T.
     SOG = 9.0kn.
c   Distance 8.8M ÷ SOG 9.0kn x 60 = 59mins.
     ETA = 1130 + 59mins = 1229 BST.

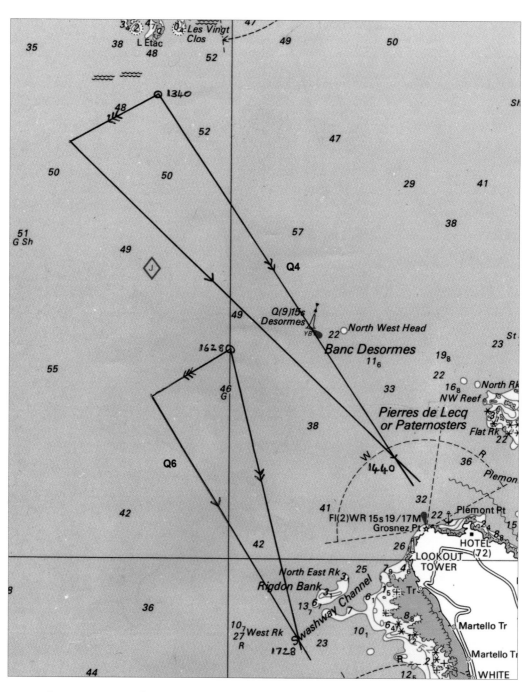

FIG **A7.4** Course to Steer Q7.4 & 7.6.

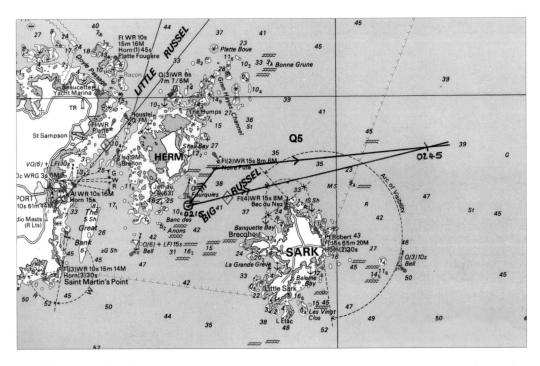

FIG **A7.5** Course to Steer Q7.5.

Answers • 8

8 Dead Reckoning and Estimated Position

8.1

See Fig A8.1.

DR position = 170°T 0.9M from Le Légué Safe Water Mark.

8.2

See Fig A8.1.

a   48°36′.1N 02° 47′.1W.
b   COG = 241°T.
c   SOG = 3.7kn.

8.3

See Fig A8.2.

325°T 2.35M.

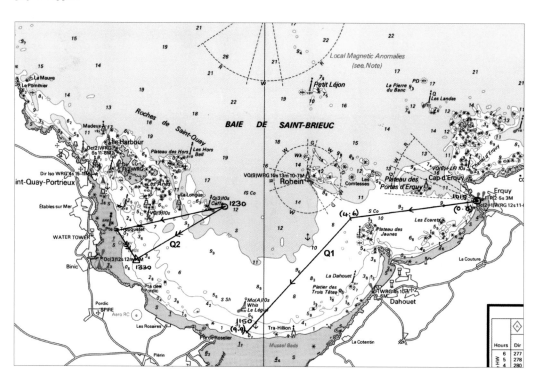

FIG **A8.1** DR & EP Q8.1 & 8.2.

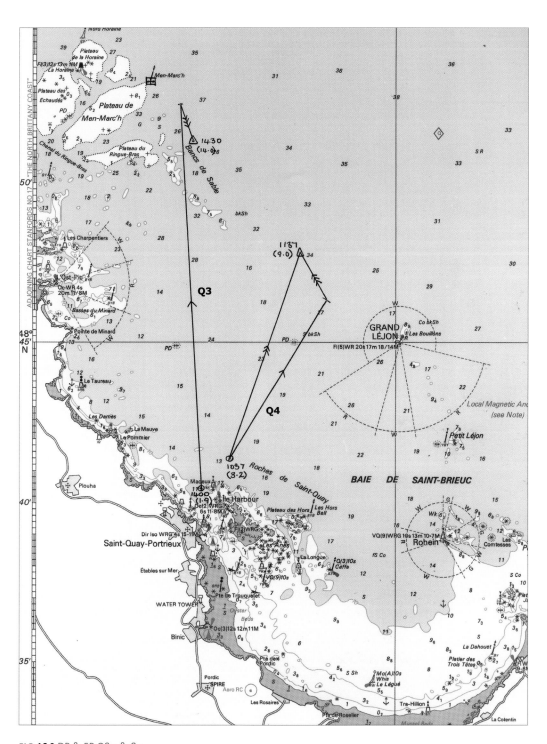

FIG **A8.2** DR & EP Q8.3 & 8.4.

8.4

See Fig A8.2.

30 September:

a   HW Dover 1307 BST. Range 6.1, springs.
b   HW hour 1237–1337. HW −2 = 1037–1137 = 330°T 1.7kn.
c   EP 48° 47'.7N 02° 44'.4W.
d   COG = 019°T. SOG = 6.8kn.

8.5

See Fig A8.3.

a   49°06'.7N 02°51'.0W.
b   No, the yacht will not clear the area.

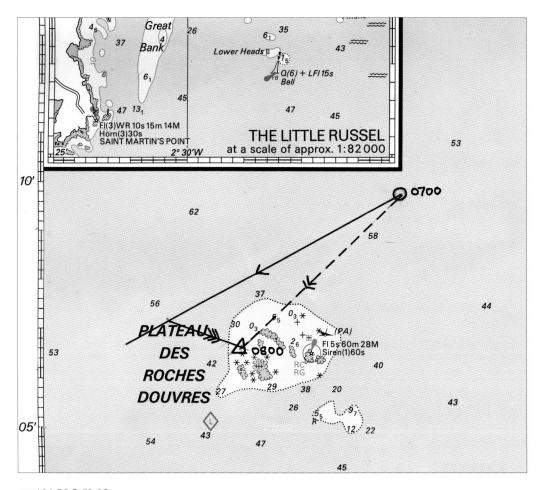

FIG A8.3 DR & EP Q8.5.

8.6

See Fig A8.5 (page 64).

23 November:

HW St Helier 1608 UTC. Range 6.9m, mid range
HW hour 1538–1638

From ® HW −2 1338–1438 = 097°T. Spring 2.3kn. Neap 1.0kn. Mid = 1.65kn
     ® HW −1 1438–1538 = 094°T. Spring 1.5kn. Neap 0.7kn. Mid = 1.1kn

1st leg   060°M = 057°T distance 4.3M
2nd leg   095°M = 092°T distance 7.6M

Position of EP = 48°41'.7N 02°16'.7W

8.7

See Fig A8.5 (page 64).

14 October:

HW St Helier 0723 BST. Range 9.5m, springs

a   To the east of Grand Léjon lighthouse.

b   Heading 185° Compass
     Deviation   +1°E
     _____
                        186°M
     Variation   −3°W
     _____
                        183°M
     Leeway   +5°
     To plot 188°T (See Fig A8.4)

c   HW hour 0653–0753 BST.
     ◇ HW +3 0953–1053 BST = 310°T 2.1kn.

d   To port. At the closest point it will be 0.7M from the
     yacht.

e   The yacht is tracking directly to the post. Leeway may
     well have been underestimated and the strength of the
     stream will decrease within the bay, so it would be wise
     to put in a short tack once it is certain that Petit Léjon
     has been cleared.

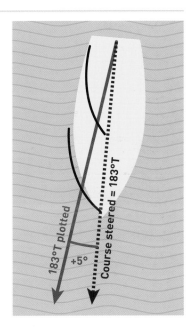

FIG A8.4 Allowance for leeway.

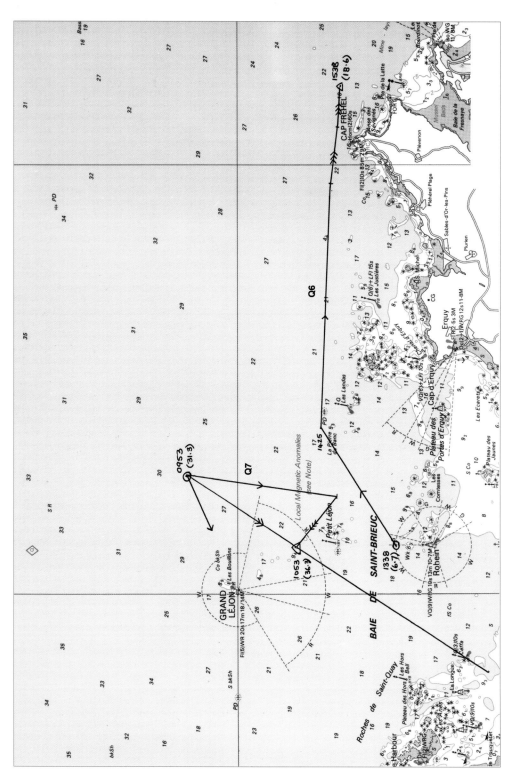

FIG **A8.5** DR & EP Q8.6 & 8.7.

9 Instrumentation and GPS

9.1

a The paddle wheel may be encrusted with weed and barnacles. A yacht that is heeled over in a rough sea may have the paddle clear of the water on occasions. The same may happen to a fast motor cruiser when the hull bangs down onto waves.

b A log that under-reads would give the greatest concern as the destination (and possibly a rocky outcrop) would be reached sooner than expected.

9.2

a No 2 is correct. If the radar is interfaced to an electronic compass, the radar picture will be stabilised so that it does not swing to and fro as the boat yaws. Radar plotting becomes more difficult with an erratic contact.

b A display in 'North Up' mode means that the radar picture is aligned so that the picture looks like the chart, with north at the top of the display. This is only possible when the radar is interfaced with an electronic compass.

c This is a very dangerous thing to do. If the 'sea clutter' control is turned to remove all the white speckles, a weak contact may also be removed from the screen. Use the control with great caution and, if using an older set, turn the clutter control to its minimum setting before switching off.

d The formula for calculating the radar horizon is:

2.25 x square root of the antenna height in metres (the square root of 4 = 2).

The boat in the example will therefore have a radar horizon of 4.5M.

e Yes. The antenna with a narrow beam will give better target discrimination. Long antennas give a narrow beam width, but it is not often possible to mount a very long antenna on a small boat.

f The hull of the small steel boat will give a good radar return, whereas the radar beam will pass straight through the glassfibre hull.

9.3

When the depth sounder pulse hits a soft and squashy seabed it penetrates the softest mud at the surface rather than bouncing the pulse back to the receiver. This makes it difficult to measure the depth accurately.

A propeller churning through water causes turbulence and many air bubbles. The sounder pulse bounces off the bubbles, not the seabed. It is common for sounders to read zero as a boat passes through the wake of power driven craft.

9.4

Most sounders have deep and shallow alarms that can be set to warn the crew if the boat moves position. Once allowance for the rise and fall of the tide has been made the alarms can be set.

9.5

The GPS antenna gives a better performance if it is mounted low down on the craft. The tall mast of a yacht moves through a great arc when in a rough sea, which can cause inaccuracies in the displayed position.

9.6

a   False. Modern sets have 12 channels and can use that number of satellites to get a position.

b   True.

c   True. All British Admiralty charts are now based on the WGS 84 datum rather than one of the many national datums. Older British charts were based on the European Datum 1950 or the Ordnance Survey of Great Britain 1936.

d   False. Satellite Differential refines the GPS position, resulting in an accuracy to within 3m 95 per cent of the time. It achieves this by using ground stations, whose precise location is known, to calculate the error in their displayed GPS position. The correction signal is then sent to the

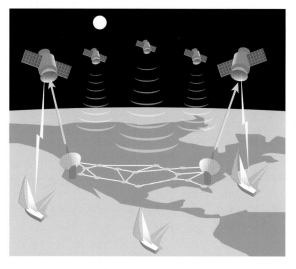

FIG **A9.1** Satellite Differential GPS.

EGNOS and WAAS satellites, from whom the correction signal can be received by mariners. These complicated calculations are handled automatically by modern GPS receivers (see Fig A9.1).

9.7

This means that the Horizontal Dilution of Position is giving a high reading on the GPS display. This tells the navigator that the position is not the most accurate one – a good number is low at around 1.4.

9.8

a   Cross track error.

b   Time to go (to waypoint).

c   Speed over ground.

d   Velocity made good.

9.9

b and **c** apply to vector charts. The remaining two – **a** and **d** – apply to raster charts.

10 Pilotage

10.1

a A transit line using the right-hand edge of Burhou Island and Great Nannel clears both Ozzard Rock and the Corbet group. Alternatively, a clearing bearing on the right-hand edge of Burhou of no less than 008°M gives a similar clearance if Great Nannel cannot be identified.

b Use the transit already marked on the chart, but have the handbearing compass handy to check the bearing of 083°M on the end of the breakwater in case the Chateau is not easily visible.

10.2

See Fig A10.1.

a The boat is somewhere in the middle of the Paternoster Rocks where there are many rocks that cover and uncover.

b One possible explanation is that the compass could have been damaged or a mobile phone may have been wedged near it, but this deviation would have become apparent on the GPS display as the cross track error increased.

  The most likely cause is an error in entering the waypoint. If 49°17'.6N were entered instead of 49°16'.7N, the boat would be led straight across the rocks.

c The skipper should have drawn the route on the chart so that the bearing and distance between each waypoint could be checked. It would also have been wise to take a back bearing on Sorel Point lighthouse as the Desormes Buoy would probably not be visible at almost 4M distant.

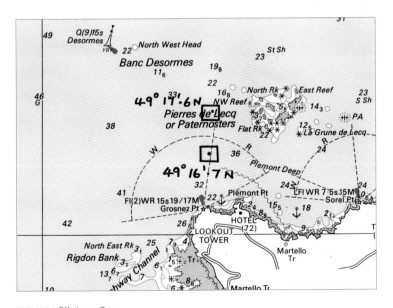

FIG **A10.1** Pilotage Q10.2.

10.3

Illustration **a**. See Fig A10.2.

FIG A10.2 Leading lights.

10.4

a Yes. The eastern end of the island is closed to the public from 1 April to 30 June. It is now July, so a visit is possible.

b Yes. The islands are not considered to be a port of entry and the boat is entering French territory from outside the EU (Jersey). The boat must visit an entry port, ie Granville or St Malo, before going on to Îles Chausey.

c There is no harbourmaster and no VHF channel in use.

d Yes, there is a bar.

e 7.2m. The channel dries 4.4m + 1.3m draught + 1.5m clearance.

10.5

All movements are prohibited except for the large ship that is departing.

10.6

Sunday 20 June:

a HW St Malo 0831 FStanT.
HW Granville +5mins = 0936 FSumT.
Access to marina = HW −2½ to HW +3½ = 0706 to 1306.

b A sharp turning out of the marina hides other vessels from view.

c No, entry and exit must be under power.

d On a digital display on top of the southern breakwater.

e Shallowest part of Granville entrance channel dries 2.0m.
Access from marina is at 0706.

HW St Malo FStanT	0831	10.8m	LW 2.7m	Mid range
Differences for Granville	+0005	+0.6m	+0.2m	
	0836	11.4m	2.9m	
Plus 1 hour for FSumT	0936			

Height of tide at 0706 = 7.6m
Depth of water over the drying 2.0 patch = 5.6m

f Yes, it is possible.

HW St Malo (FSumT)	0931	10.8m	LW 2.7m

Time of arrival = 1400 = HW + 4½ hours
Height of tide = 5.2m
Sill dries 2.0m therefore depth over the sill at 1400 = 3.2m
Depth required = Draught 1.8m plus clearance of 1.0m = 2.8m

g Channel 9.

h Yes, there are waiting buoys outside Bas Sablons marina.

11 Collision Regulations

11.1

a 'A vessel not under command' cannot manoeuvre according to the Rules because of some special circumstance and is therefore unable to keep out of the way of other vessels.

b 'A sailing vessel' is any vessel under sail, provided that propelling machinery is not being used.

11.2

The heading must be at right angles (see Fig A11.1). This means that the crossing vessel is presenting a beam-on aspect to shipping within the lane and reaches the far side of the lane more quickly than the vessel on a right-angled ground track.

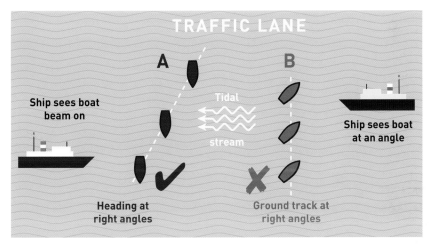

FIG **A11.1** Crossing shipping lanes.

11.3

a Yacht A is the give way vessel as, although it is on the same tack as B, it is to windward. The skipper should ease sheets and bear away to pass astern of B.

b Yacht B, on port tack, should give way to Yacht A on starboard tack. The skipper should either tack onto a parallel course or ease sheets to bear away round the stern of A.

c Motorboat A gives way to motorboat B. It should sound one short blast on the horn and alter course to starboard to pass behind B. (Boat A can see B's red light. The rhyme 'If to starboard red appear it is your duty to keep clear' is a good one to remember.)

d Both A and B should give way. Each should sound one short blast and alter course to starboard. (*Note: Only power driven craft give a sound signal when altering course.*)

e Yacht B is the give way vessel as it is overtaking A. The helmsman should pass astern of boat A. Remember that ANY vessel overtaking another becomes the give way vessel, even a vessel not under command!

f Power driven vessel A is the give way vessel. She must sound the appropriate sound signal and alter course to avoid vessel B, or stop and let B pass ahead.

11.4

No. The words 'Right of Way' do not appear anywhere in the IRPCS. It is the duty of all vessels to avoid a collision.

11.5

No. Rule 5 requires a lookout to be kept at all times by all available means. A visual watch is therefore mandatory.

11.6

Vessels under 20m in length and sailing vessels.

11.7

International code flag A should be hoisted when a diver is down (see Fig A11.2).

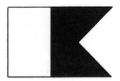

FIG A11.2 International code flag A.

11.8

a   At anchor.
b   Restricted in its ability to manoeuvre.
c   Motorsailing.
d   Aground.
e   Constrained by draught.
f   Gear extending more than 150m horizontally from a fishing vessel.
g   Fishing or trawling.
h   Not under command.
i   Length of tow exceeds 200m.

11.9

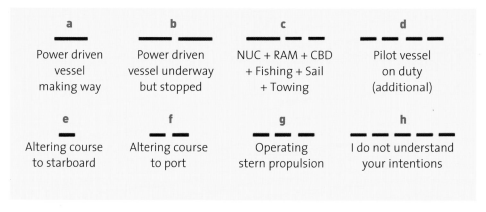

a	b	c	d
▬	▬ ▬	▬ ▬ ▬	▬ ▬ ▬
Power driven vessel making way	Power driven vessel underway but stopped	NUC + RAM + CBD + Fishing + Sail + Towing	Pilot vessel on duty (additional)

e	f	g	h
▬ ▬	▬ ▬	▬ ▬ ▬	▬ ▬ ▬ ▬
Altering course to starboard	Altering course to port	Operating stern propulsion	I do not understand your intentions

FIG A11.3 Sound signals and their meanings.

11.10

A Power driven vessel (PDV), seen from ahead, probably more than 50m in length, underway.

B Not under command (NUC), underway but stopped, length and aspect unknown.

C Sailing vessel, underway/making way, starboard aspect, length unknown.
(*Although this looks like the high tricolour lantern of a boat under 20m in length, it could be a large high-sided sail training vessel with a sidelight.*)

D PDV, underway/making way, engaged in towing, seen from ahead. It is *either* under 50m in length with a tow of more than 200m, *or* more than 50m with a tow of under 200m.

E Restricted in its ability to manoeuvre (RAM), under 50m in length, making way, port aspect.
(*Note that NUC, RAM and fishing/trawling turn their sidelights and stern light OFF when they are not making way through the water.*)

F A stern light of a vessel of any length, *or* an all-round anchor light of a vessel under 50m, *or* under oars, *or* a small PDV, under 7m and under 7kn.

G Pilot vessel, underway/making way, starboard aspect.

H Trawling, under 50m in length, making way, port aspect.

I Fishing, stopped (making no way), aspect unknown, no gear more than 150m.

J Constrained by draught, probably more than 50m in length, underway/making way, starboard aspect.

K Fishing, making way, no gear extending, no length indication, head on.

L At anchor, probably more than 50m in length, port aspect. (*When at anchor the light at the bow is higher than the aft light.*)

11.11

a Low sidelights, stern light and steaming light. (As the boat is less than 12m in length, the stern light and steaming light may be combined in one light at the masthead.)

b Sidelights, stern light and steaming light. (The last two may be combined.)

c An all-round white light and, if practicable, sidelights. The boat is under 7m in length and has a maximum speed of under 7 knots.

Answers · 12

12 Meteorology

12.1

a	Slight	Wave height 0.5m to 1.25m
b	Moving steadily	A weather system moving at 15 to 25 knots.
c	Rough	Waves of between 2.5 and 4 metres.
d	Gale force	Beaufort Force 8 (34-40 knots).
e	Imminent	Within 6 hours of issue of the warning.
f	Moderate	Visibility of between 2 and 5 miles.
g	Cyclonic	The centre of low pressure will pass through the sea area with the wind altering direction as expected in a depression.
h	Poor	Visibility between 1,000 metres and 2 miles.
i	Fair	No significant precipitation.
j	Soon	Between 6 and 12 hours from issue of the warning.
k	Veering	Wind will alter in a clockwise direction.
l	Strong wind	Winds are expected to reach Force 6 warning.

12.2

a The wind would be circulating in a clockwise direction (see Fig A12.1).

b Light.

c Stable conditions, but with surface heating in the summer causing some instability (sea breezes along the coast) during the day.

d West South West and light.

12.3

To the west. Buys Ballot's law says, 'if you stand with your back to the wind in the northern hemisphere, then the area of low pressure is on your left-hand side.'

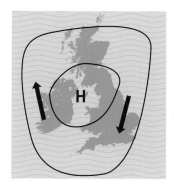

FIG A12.1 Clockwise wind circulation.

12.4

a Force 4 (11–16kn).

b Force 6 (22–27kn).

12.5

a It is cumulonimbus cloud in photo A. It is cirrus cloud in photo B.

b Cloud B. This cirrus cloud is hooked on the strong upper wind and is found ahead of a warm front.

c Cloud A. Strong, gusty winds are found under these clouds. Cumulus clouds will decrease in size and frequency as the weather settles and showers die out.

12.6

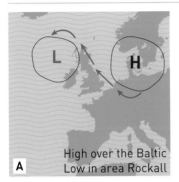

A High over the Baltic
   Low in area Rockall

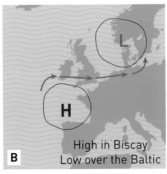

B High in Biscay
   Low over the Baltic

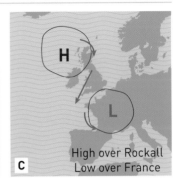

C High over Rockall
   Low over France

FIG **A12.2**

A SE strong (Fig A12.2A).
B W moderate (Fig A12.2B).
C NE or ENE strong (Fig A12.2C).

12.7

Sea fog
a When there is warm damp air blowing over a cold surface such as the sea.
b In the late spring and early summer when the sea is still cold and the warm tropical air comes up from the south.
c A wing strength of over Force 5 should lift the fog off the sea surface to give low stratus cloud, or a change to a polar air-stream will clear it.
d Wind and tidal stream invariably strengthen around headlands where the sea bed is uneven. The water is roughened which causes turbulence in the air above it. This turbulence helps to cool the air below the dew point and fog forms. In less turbulent areas the fog may not form.

Radiation fog
e This type of fog typically forms in autumn and winter when the land cools quickly.
f Yes, when the air is heated it can hold more water vapour invisibly and the fog disperses on all but the worst days.

12.8

a Southeasterly or south-southeasterly.
b An occlusion (where the warm and colds fronts merge together). The warm air has left the surface and now lies on top of the cooler air.
c The pressure will be falling in area Forties.
d Sea area Plymouth is in the warm sector, and the visibility will be poor with intermittent rain and drizzle.
e Stratus and nimbostratus with altostratus above it.
f Good visibility, noticeably cooler than of late, occasional cumulonimbus or cumulus clouds, but improving all the time. Barometric pressure will probably be rising slowly.

12.9

a Your diagram should look similar to that in Fig A12.3.

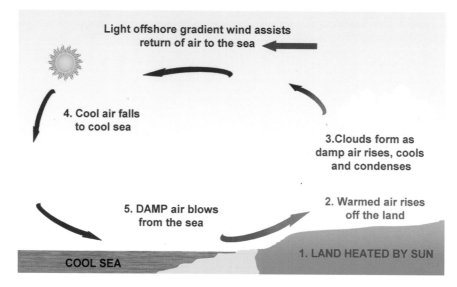

FIG **A12.3**

b The wind will tend to veer during the day.
c The breeze will be strongest in the mid afternoon when the land is well heated and the greatest circulation has been set up.
d As the sun sets the land will cool and the breeze will die. A land breeze may blow lightly seaward but if not the conditions will be calm.

13 Safety and Communications

13.1

a
- Open the cover, which is either red or labelled 'Distress'.
- Press the red button once and, if there is time, select the type of distress situation from a list of categories.
- Press the red button for 5 seconds or until the 'Distress alert sent' message appears on the display.

b The casualty's MMSI (identification number) and, provided the set is interfaced with a GPS, the time and the boat's position in latitude and longitude. If selected, the nature of distress.

c Digitally first, and then by voice after the voice Mayday.

d 15 seconds to allow time for the digital acknowledgement to be sent by the coast station.

e

> Mayday, Mayday, Mayday.
> This is Motor Cruiser *Sinking Feeling, Sinking Feeling, Sinking Feeling.*
> MMSI 234002345. Call sign 2ZXY4
> Mayday *Sinking Feeling.* MMSI 234002345 Call sign 2ZXY4
> My position is 50° 10'.4N 001° 18'.6W.
> Holed and sinking.
> Require immediate assistance.
> 4 persons on board. Abandoning to liferaft.
> Over.

f The digital signal has the greater range.

13.2

a Normally the helicopter will make an approach on the port side of the casualty as the pilot and the door are on the right-hand side of the aircraft. However, a powerless, wallowing craft may not head into wind, in which case the helicopter will try to approach into wind as the short mast of a motor cruiser does not restrict the approach angle.

b The crew will be told:

  i   that either a weighted line or the diver on a wire will be lowered to the deck.

  ii not to attach the line to the vessel.

  iii to take control of the line and to assist the diver onto the deck.

  (*Note: In the case of the crew of Sinking Feeling, they are most likely to be sent up into the helicopter in pairs in a rescue strop with the diver remaining on the craft until everyone is safe.*)

c A handheld red pinpoint flare or an orange smoke.

d A parachute flare. Helicopters do not appreciate an attempt to shoot them down!

Answers · 13

FIG **A13.1** Rescuer on the way.

13.3

a Channel 16.
b Channel 6.
c Channel 67.
d Channel 80.

13.4

a Gale and strong wind warnings.
   Shipping forecast extracts of local areas, inshore waters forecasts and 2 day forecasts.
   Information on firing times at ranges (Gunfax) and activity in submarine exercise areas
   (Subfax).
b ii Three hourly with a new inshore waters forecast every six hours.

13.5

a This refers to the 'Angle of Vanishing Stability' – the angle above which the boat no longer
   regains an upright position and finds it easier to turn upside down. Those craft with a high
   AVS can heel to a greater angle before they lose stability, and are therefore more suitable for
   comfortable, safe ocean cruising where it is difficult to find shelter in heavy weather. They
   may not be as fast as one with a low AVS.

b This is an Emergency Position Indicating Radio Beacon (EPIRB) which, when activated, uses the frequency of 406MHzto send a signal to a receiving station via a satellite. The ground station contacts Falmouth Coastguard who maintain the national registry of EPIRB serial numbers, so that the casualty may easily be identified. Falmouth Coastguard then alert local rescue services to help the casualty.

If you acquire a secondhand EPIRB you should inform HM Coastguard at Falmouth about the change of ownership – this is a legal requirement.

13.6

a A red parachute flare (bottom left of Fig 13.3 on page 31) that can ascend to about 300m.
b An orange smoke signal (right of Fig 13.3 on page 31).
c A handheld pinpoint red flare (top left of Fig 13.3 on page 31).

13.7

Between three or four years depending on the time of year that the pack is purchased.

13.8

a The torch bearer is telling you that you are running into danger.
b You should stop and/or retrace your route while you sort things out.

FIG **A13.2** An EPIRB.

13.9

The aircraft is telling the skipper that his message has been understood.

Answers ▪ 14

14 Planning and Making Passages

Passage planning does not always have a definitive answer – the answers given here are one option considered to give a successful passage. If your answers differ a little, they are probably not wrong, just a different interpretation.

Passage 1

14.1

Sunday 5 September:

a St Helier HW 1054 BST. Range 6.3m, mid range.

b St Helier HW –3hrs to HW +3hrs = 0754 to 1354.

c Yes. La Collette basin has 24hr access with a 1.8m minimum depth.

d Distance is approximately 37M. Passage time approx 1hr 30mins in calm sea.

e HW Dover 1558 BST.

f The stream is favourable for the whole length of the passage from 1130 to 1330. Before 1130 there is an adverse stream along the south coast of Jersey, and after 1330 there is a counter current off Diélette.

g Yes, it is restricted by the depths in the outer harbour but mostly at springs. The narrative for Diélette says that it is dredged to CD +0.5m, but the chart shows it dredged to datum. We must therefore assume that it dries 0.5m, which is the worst case. As 5 September is mid range, we can look at the differences data:

St Malo MLWN = 4.2m less 0.7m at Diélette = 3.5m
St Malo MLWS = 1.5m less 0.3m at Diélette = 1.2m
Take a mid range Figure between these two = 2.35m

The cruiser is therefore likely to float at all states of the tide on 5 September provided that the recommended route is used once inside the breakwater.

h HW Dover 1558 BST. Diélette HW is HW Dover –4hrs 30mins = 1128 BST.
Access is HW +/–3hrs = 0828 to 1428 BST

i Dangers:

- Ships and ferries leaving St Helier. Watch the traffic lights.
- Rocks at St Helier entrance.
- Rough water off Point Corbière.
- Rough water off Rigdon Bank on the northwest corner of Jersey.
- The Paternoster Rocks off the north coast of Jersey.
- Local magnetic anomalies affecting the compass.
- Rocky bank to the northeast of Diélette entrance.
- Traffic leaving round the corner of the breakwater at Diélette.

j Close to 1130, which will give ample time to benefit from the fair stream.

k Tune to Channel 18 VHF to obtain information about wind speed and direction at St Helier Pierheads.

14.2

Waypoint 1 to 2	277°T	4.8M
Waypoint 2 to 3	353°T	4.0M
Waypoint 3 to 4	030°T	4.9M
Waypoint 4 to 5	041°T	19.4M
Waypoint 5 to 6	070°T	1.5M

14.3

See Fig A14.1.

a 49° 29'.0N 02° 02'.5W.
b HW Dover 1558 BST. Mid range.
HW hour = 1528–1628. HW −3 = 1228–1328.
The stream charts show that two arrows and rates cover the passage area.

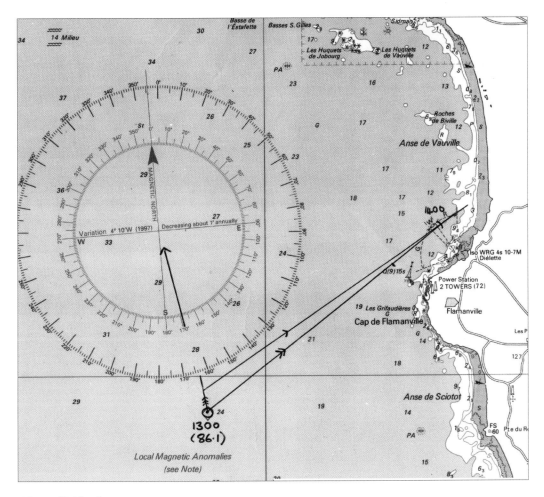

FIG **A14.1** Plot for Q14.3.

The average direction and rate for mid range = 348°T 1.5kn (20 mins 0.5M).
Course to steer = 057°T + 3°W variation = 060°M − 1°E deviation = 059°C.

(*Note: A 20 minute tidal vector has been plotted, ie both boat speed and rate of stream have been divided by three – same triangle but smaller scale.*)

c   Formula for ETA at the buoy:

Distance to go ÷ distance covered in 20mins x 20 = elapsed time
6.6M ÷ 8.3M x 20 = 16mins run. ETA = 1316 BST.

14.4

Yes it does, there is a 30 ton crane although you may not be very lucky on a Sunday afternoon!

Passage 2

14.5

Wednesday 4 August

HW St Peter Port 0905 BST 9.2m:

a   Use the table in extract 14 at the back of this book to give heights over the marina sill.
Water required = 1.9m draught + 0.5m clearance = 2.4m.
Depth over the sill at HW −2½hrs = 2.08m and at HW −2hrs = 3.05m.
There is sufficient depth at HW +/−2hrs 15mins = 0650 to 1120 BST.

b   Visitors may wait on the waiting pontoon or, if additional depth is required, on pontoons 1 to 5 (see the harbour chart in Extract 13 at the back of the book).

14.6

a   Distance to the southwest corner of Jersey is approximately 19½ miles and 34 miles more to Granville.

b   It will take just over 3hrs to complete the first part provided that the wind is not force 5 on the nose – when it would take longer. A further 5¾ hrs will be needed for the second part (excluding the tidal stream).

14.7

a   St Malo is the standard port for Granville and HW St Malo is at 2158 BST.

b   HW Granville is at HW St Malo +5 minutes = 2203 BST.

c   Access to Granville Marina is HW Granville −2½hrs to HW +3½hrs = 1933 to 0133 (5 August).

d   HW Dover = 1435 BST. Springs.

e   The best time to arrive, thinking of the stream alone, would be by HW Dover +4½ hrs (1905) as all the tidal arrows point to Granville, but the marina would not be open at that time. Arriving at HW Dover +5½hrs would just about be acceptable as there is under 1kn of stream against us on the run into the port. After that, the stream picks up against us.

14.8

a   The latest time to leave the marina is 1120, so exit before then is essential.
b   If the wind is still in the south the passage to the Corbière corner will be a beat, so it would be wise to leave a little before then even though the stream outside the harbour is setting north.

If the wind has already veered, then we can wait in the outer harbour until the stream turns south at about 1230. We should then cover the 20M to southwest Jersey by 1600 to take slack or weak favourable stream along the south Jersey coast – nicely on schedule.

First thoughts are that there will be little stream advantage during the first 20M because it is a cross-stream, but once south of Jersey the strong favourable stream should be carried to Granville – and any time lost earlier can be made up.

14.9

A cold front is passing over the area. This is a typical forecast – a veer in the wind, increased visibility and rain turning to showers after the front has passed.

On passage

14.10

See Fig A14.2.

Wednesday 4 August:

HW St Helier 0958 BST. Springs.
HW hour 0928–1028

◇ HW + 3 1228–1328 = 004°T   0.7kn ½hr 0.35M
◇ HW + 4 1328–1428 = 282°T   0.7kn ½hr 0.35M

Course:	135°C
Deviation	+5°E
Magnetic	140°M
Leeway	−10°
Variation	−3°W
Plotted	127°T

a   EP 49° 22'.6N 02° 21'.4W.
b   The difference in the two positions could be for a number of reasons. The tide may have turned early, the leeway may have been over-estimated, or perhaps the helmsman finds sailing to windward difficult.

14.11

See Fig A14.3.

HW Dover 1435 BST HW hour 1405–1505
HW Dover +5 = 1905–2005. 100°T. 1.9kn. Boat speed 7kn.

a   Course to steer = 142°T + 3°W = 145°M −4°E = 141°C.
b   SOG = 8.6kn.

Answers · 14

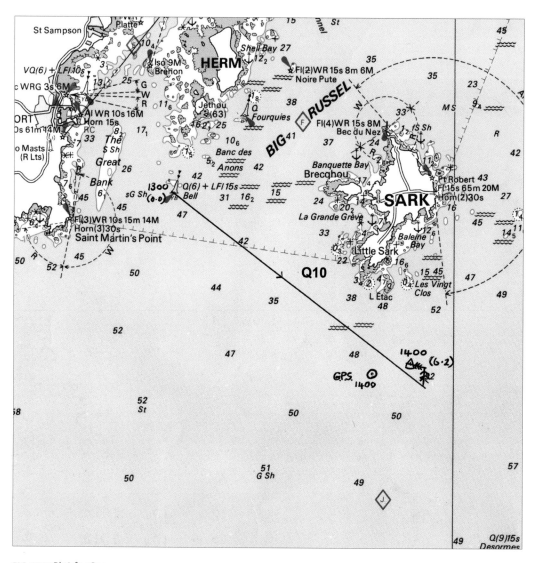

FIG A14.2 Plot for Q14.10.

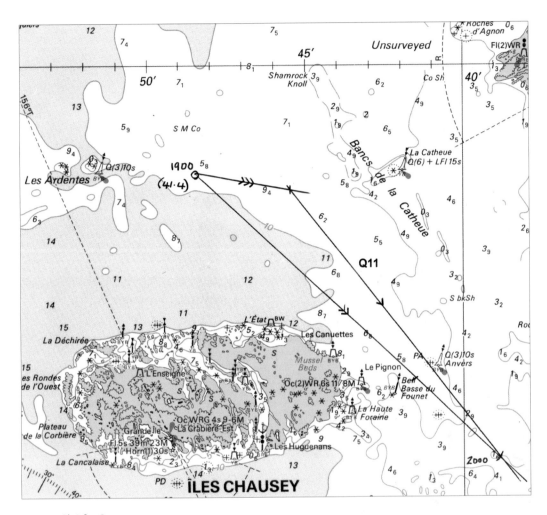

14.12

a The dangers are: rocks and lobster pots off Pointe du Roc, and traffic coming round the blind bend outside the marina.

b The skipper can check depth calculations by sighting the illuminated tidal height display board on the southern harbour wall.

Chartwork test papers **answers**

15 Test Paper 1

15.1

See Fig A15.1.

Position at 1010 UTC is 49° 41'.0N 02° 09'.7°W.

15.2

See Fig A15.1.

Tuesday 2 November:

HW St Helier 0842 UTC. Range 6.5m, close to mid range
HW hour 0812–0912 UTC

ⒷHW +2 1012–1112 031°T 4.2kn (spring) 2.0kn (neap) 3.1kn (mid)

a   Course to steer 080°T + 3°W = 083°M.
b   Slack at 1212 UTC, and clearly unfavourable by 1312 UTC (HW +5).

15.3

See Fig A15.3

Thursday 21 October:

HW St Helier 1226 BST. Range 4.2m, neaps
HW hour 1156–1256

ⒸHW −5 0656–0756 203°T 1.4kn
ⒸHW −4 0756–0856 172°T 1.0kn

1st Course: 270°C − 4°W deviation − 3°W variation + 10° leeway = 273°T
2nd Course: 170°C + 2°E deviation − 3°W variation − 10° leeway = 159°T

EP at 0800 = 49° 35'.1N 02° 29'.7W
EP at 0900 = 49° 30'.2N 02° 27'.0W

15.4

Saturday 25 September:

a   Cherbourg FStanT Range 3.2m

Cherbourg	HW 0625	5.4m	LW 1300	2.2m
Difference	+0103	+0.2m	+0052	0.0m
Barfleur FSumT	0828	5.6m	1452	2.2m

b   See Fig A15.2. From Cherbourg curve with data for Barfleur:
Height of tide at 1055 FSumT = 4.5m.
c   Fall to LW (2.2m) = 2.3m.
Depth of water in which to anchor:
Fall 2.3m + Draught 1.8m + Clearance 1.0m = 5.1m.

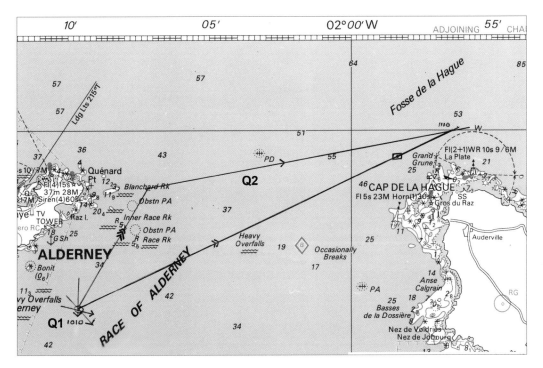

FIG **A15.1** Test Paper 1 Q15.1 & 15.2.

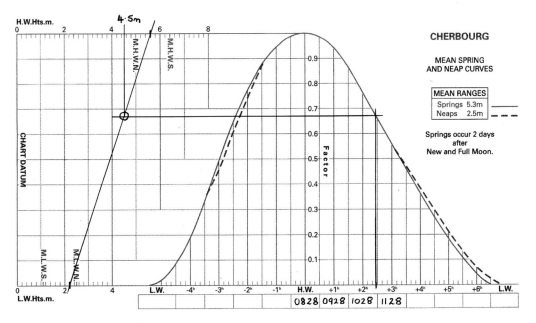

FIG **A15.2** Test Paper 1 Q15.4b.

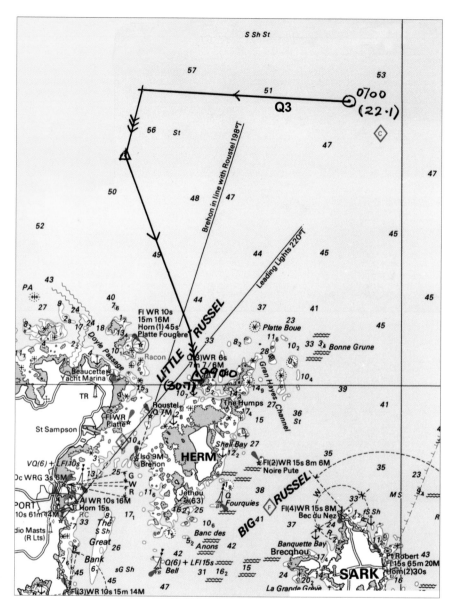

16 Test Paper 2

16.1

See Fig A16.2.

The position at 1450 = 49°16'.3N 02°06.6W.

16.2

See Fig A16.2.

Sunday 12 September.

Course to plot = 023° – 1°W deviation – 3°W variation = 019°T.

a HW St Helier 1818 BST. Range 6.7, mid range.
HW hour 1748–1848.
◈ HW –3 1448–1548 = 117°T 3.0kn (spring) 1.2kn (neap).
It is mid range, which = 2.1kn; ½hr = 1.05M.
EP at 1520 = 49°21'.4N 02°02'.1W.

b 1.0M

c Distance 3.2M ÷ SOG 12.0kn x 60 = 16mins + 1450 = 1506 BST.

d The skipper could:

- draw a clearing bearing of 215°M on the TV mast which would give 1M clearance;
- insert a waypoint north of the rocks and steer to keep the waypoint on a safe and steady bearing, or draw a clearing bearing from the waypoint.

16.3

See Fig A16.3

Thursday 14 October:

HW Dover 1151 BST. Range 5.9m, springs
Distance to go = 9M, therefore approx 2hrs at 4kn

HW hour 1121–1221
HW +3 1421–1521 149°T 2.0kn
HW +4 1521–1621 149°T 2.0kn

Course to steer (no leeway) = 190°T + 3°W = 193°M.
Aim into the SE wind to correct for leeway, so subtract 5° = 188°M.

16.4

14 November:

Range 10.0m (1st HW), 9.8m (2nd HW), springs

St Helier UTC	HW 0712	11.3m	LW	1.3m	HW 1934	11.1m
Difference	+0007	0.0m		+0.1m	+0008	0.0m
St Catherine's UTC	0719	11.3m		1.4m	1942	11.1m

From St Helier curve, the height of tide at 0925 = 8.8m

a   At 0925 the yacht is anchored in 3.0m water when the height of tide is 8.8m, so she must be anchored on a drying 5.8m beach as shown in Fig A16.1. The yacht draws 1.4m, which leaves 1.6m of water under the keel.

The tide has therefore to fall 1.6m for the yacht to ground.

Therefore the yacht grounds when the height of tide is 7.2m = 1010 UTC.

b   The tide has to fall a further 1.4m (the draught) for the yacht to dry out, ie to 5.8m.

The tidal height is 5.8m above datum at 1045 UTC.

c   Mark the new HW St Catherine's height (11.1m) on the HW line and the time of the next HW in the box at the bottom. Now calculate at what time the height of tide will rise to 7.2m when the yacht will re-float.

Answer = 1717 UTC.

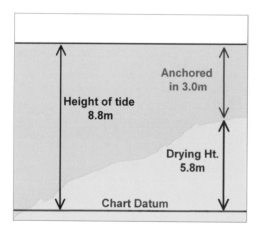

FIG A16.1 Tidal calculation for Q16.4.

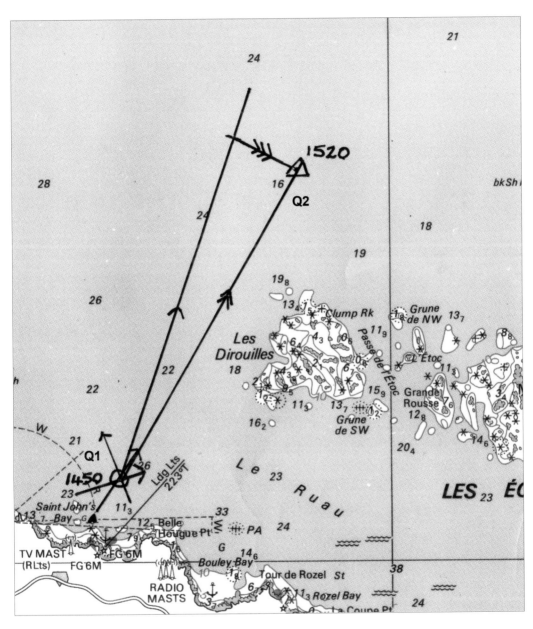

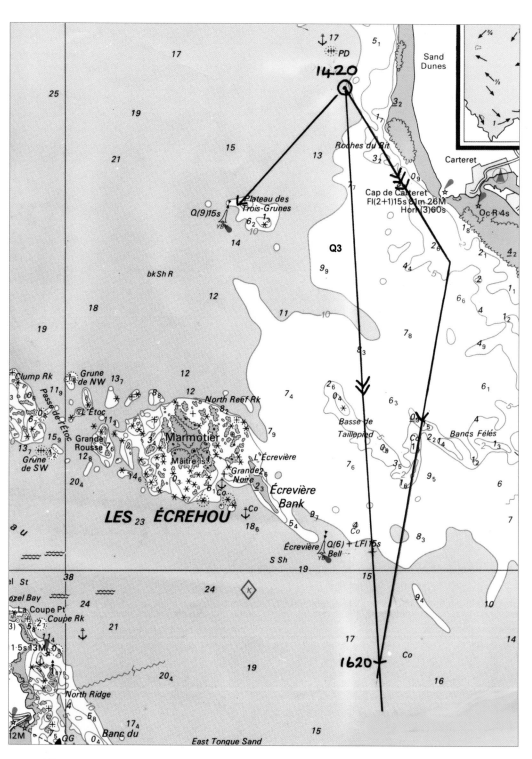

All extracts are taken from *Reeds Nautical Almanac*.

Extract 1: Dover Tide Tables – May to August

TIME ZONE (UT)	ENGLAND – DOVER	SPRING & NEAP TIDES
For Summer Time add ONE hour in **non-shaded areas**	LAT 51°07'N LONG 1°19'E — TIMES AND HEIGHTS OF HIGH AND LOW WATERS	Dates in red are SPRINGS — Dates in blue are NEAPS

MAY

Date	Day	Time m	Time m	Time m	Time m
1	SA	0300 1.7	0824 5.7	1530 1.7	2042 6.0
2	SU	0353 1.3	0908 6.1	1620 1.4	2124 6.4
3	M	0443 1.0	0947 6.4	1708 1.1	2204 6.7
4	TU	0533 0.8	1026 6.6	1754 0.9	○ 2244 6.9
5	W	0620 0.7	1105 6.8	1838 0.8	2324 7.0
6	TH	0704 0.6	1146 6.8	1920 0.7	
7	F	0007 7.0	0746 0.7	1230 6.8	2001 0.8
8	SA	0053 6.8	0827 0.8	1318 6.6	2045 1.0
9	SU	0143 6.5	0911 1.1	1412 6.3	2134 1.3
10	M	0243 6.1	1002 1.5	1513 6.0	2231 1.6
11	TU	0353 5.7	1105 1.9	1622 5.7	◐ 2343 1.8
12	W	0514 5.4	1223 2.1	1738 5.5	
13	TH	0103 1.9	0648 5.4	1340 2.0	1904 5.5
14	F	0220 1.7	0804 5.6	1450 1.8	2013 5.8
15	SA	0328 1.4	0857 5.8	1551 1.5	2104 6.0
16	SU	0426 1.2	0939 6.0	1642 1.3	2146 6.2
17	M	0513 1.1	1014 6.2	1725 1.2	2225 6.4
18	TU	0552 1.1	1048 6.3	1802 1.2	2302 6.4
19	W	0623 1.1	1121 6.3	1833 1.2	● 2336 6.4
20	TH	0650 1.2	1155 6.3	1900 1.2	
21	F	0009 6.3	0714 1.3	1228 6.3	1926 1.2
22	SA	0038 6.2	0740 1.3	1258 6.2	1955 1.3
23	SU	0104 6.0	0810 1.5	1325 6.1	2028 1.5
24	M	0131 5.9	0843 1.6	1354 5.9	2104 1.7
25	TU	0207 5.7	0922 1.8	1436 5.7	2147 1.9
26	W	0258 5.5	1007 2.0	1533 5.5	2239 2.0
27	TH	0416 5.3	1104 2.2	1647 5.4	◑ 2350 2.1
28	F	0538 5.3	1225 2.2	1800 5.4	
29	SA	0109 1.9	0644 5.4	1342 2.1	1903 5.7
30	SU	0214 1.7	0740 5.7	1443 1.8	1957 6.0
31	M	0310 1.4	0828 6.0	1539 1.5	2045 6.3

JUNE

Date	Day	Time m	Time m	Time m	Time m
1	TU	0406 1.1	0914 6.3	1633 1.2	2132 6.6
2	W	0501 0.9	0958 6.5	1726 1.0	2218 6.7
3	TH	0555 0.8	1045 6.6	1817 0.9	○ 2306 6.8
4	F	0646 0.8	1132 6.7	1906 0.8	2355 6.8
5	SA	0736 0.8	1222 6.7	1956 0.8	
6	SU	0046 6.6	0824 0.9	1314 6.6	2046 0.9
7	M	0142 6.4	0914 1.1	1407 6.4	2139 1.1
8	TU	0241 6.2	1006 1.4	1503 6.2	2234 1.3
9	W	0343 5.9	1101 1.6	1601 6.0	◐ 2333 1.5
10	TH	0449 5.6	1159 1.8	1703 5.8	
11	F	0034 1.6	0602 5.5	1300 1.9	1812 5.7
12	SA	0135 1.6	0712 5.5	1400 1.9	1922 5.7
13	SU	0235 1.6	0810 5.6	1459 1.8	2021 5.8
14	M	0334 1.6	0857 5.7	1555 1.7	2111 5.9
15	TU	0426 1.5	0940 5.9	1644 1.5	2156 6.0
16	W	0509 1.4	1019 6.0	1726 1.4	2236 6.1
17	TH	0546 1.4	1057 6.1	1802 1.4	● 2314 6.1
18	F	0618 1.4	1134 6.2	1835 1.3	2348 6.1
19	SA	0650 1.4	1209 6.2	1908 1.3	
20	SU	0021 6.1	0722 1.4	1242 6.2	1942 1.4
21	M	0053 6.0	0757 1.5	1313 6.1	2018 1.4
22	TU	0124 5.9	0833 1.6	1344 6.1	2057 1.5
23	W	0158 5.9	0912 1.6	1421 6.0	2137 1.6
24	TH	0238 5.8	0952 1.8	1505 5.9	2222 1.7
25	F	0328 5.7	1038 1.9	1558 5.8	◑ 2314 1.7
26	SA	0429 5.6	1133 2.0	1700 5.7	
27	SU	0016 1.8	0541 5.6	1242 2.0	1807 5.8
28	M	0124 1.7	0651 5.7	1353 1.9	1913 5.9
29	TU	0229 1.5	0752 5.8	1500 1.7	2013 6.1
30	W	0333 1.4	0849 6.1	1604 1.5	2110 6.3

JULY

Date	Day	Time m	Time m	Time m	Time m
1	TH	0437 1.2	0943 6.3	1706 1.2	2206 6.5
2	F	0539 1.0	1037 6.5	1805 1.0	○ 2301 6.6
3	SA	0638 0.9	1129 6.6	1901 0.9	2355 6.6
4	SU	0734 0.9	1219 6.7	1956 0.8	
5	M	0046 6.6	0825 0.9	1307 6.7	2047 0.8
6	TU	0138 6.4	0912 1.0	1355 6.6	2135 0.8
7	W	0228 6.3	0956 1.1	1443 6.5	2221 1.0
8	TH	0318 6.0	1038 1.3	1532 6.3	2305 1.2
9	F	0410 5.8	1121 1.5	1623 6.0	◐ 2351 1.5
10	SA	0505 5.6	1208 1.9	1720 5.7	
11	SU	0042 1.7	0607 5.4	1303 2.0	1823 5.6
12	M	0138 1.9	0713 5.3	1404 2.1	1932 5.5
13	TU	0238 2.0	0814 5.4	1507 2.0	2035 5.6
14	W	0337 1.9	0906 5.8	1606 1.9	2130 5.7
15	TH	0430 1.7	0956 5.8	1655 1.6	2216 5.9
16	F	0514 1.6	1037 6.0	1737 1.5	2255 6.0
17	SA	0554 1.5	1115 6.2	1815 1.4	● 2330 6.1
18	SU	0632 1.4	1149 6.3	1853 1.3	
19	M	0003 6.1	0709 1.4	1222 6.3	1930 1.3
20	TU	0036 6.1	0747 1.4	1254 6.3	2009 1.2
21	W	0107 6.1	0823 1.4	1335 6.3	2046 1.3
22	TH	0137 6.1	0859 1.4	1358 6.3	2123 1.3
23	F	0212 6.1	0934 1.5	1437 6.3	2159 1.4
24	SA	0253 6.0	1011 1.6	1521 6.2	2241 1.5
25	SU	0342 5.9	1056 1.7	1615 6.0	◑ 2331 1.7
26	M	0444 5.7	1153 1.9	1722 5.8	
27	TU	0037 1.8	0606 5.5	1310 2.1	1840 5.7
28	W	0155 1.8	0730 5.6	1431 2.0	1958 5.8
29	TH	0311 1.7	0841 5.8	1547 1.7	2109 6.0
30	F	0425 1.5	0943 6.1	1657 1.4	2212 6.3
31	SA	0534 1.2	1038 6.4	1801 1.1	○ 2308 6.5

AUGUST

Date	Day	Time m	Time m	Time m	Time m
1	SU	0635 1.0	1126 6.6	1859 0.8	2357 6.6
2	M	0729 0.9	1211 6.8	1951 0.6	
3	TU	0041 6.6	0815 0.8	1254 6.8	2037 0.6
4	W	0123 6.5	0855 0.8	1335 6.8	2117 0.7
5	TH	0203 6.4	0930 1.0	1417 6.7	2153 0.9
6	F	0243 6.2	1002 1.2	1458 6.4	2226 1.2
7	SA	0326 5.9	1033 1.5	1542 6.1	◑ 2300 1.5
8	SU	0414 5.6	1107 1.9	1631 5.8	2341 1.9
9	M	0512 5.3	1154 2.2	1731 5.4	
10	TU	0037 2.2	0620 5.2	1307 2.4	1843 5.2
11	W	0150 2.4	0734 5.2	1426 2.4	2001 5.3
12	TH	0300 2.2	0842 5.4	1534 2.1	2110 5.5
13	F	0400 2.0	0936 5.7	1629 1.8	2159 5.8
14	SA	0451 1.7	1018 6.0	1715 1.5	2236 6.0
15	SU	0535 1.5	1052 6.2	1756 1.3	2308 6.2
16	M	0615 1.4	1125 6.4	1836 1.2	● 2340 6.3
17	TU	0654 1.3	1156 6.5	1915 1.1	
18	W	0011 6.3	0730 1.2	1228 6.5	1952 1.1
19	TH	0041 6.2	0805 1.2	1259 6.6	2027 1.0
20	F	0111 6.4	0838 1.2	1332 6.6	2100 1.1
21	SA	0144 6.4	0910 1.3	1408 6.6	2133 1.2
22	SU	0223 6.3	0944 1.4	1450 6.4	2210 1.4
23	M	0309 6.0	1026 1.7	1541 6.1	◑ 2257 1.8
24	TU	0409 5.7	1121 2.0	1651 5.7	
25	W	0003 2.1	0543 5.3	1242 2.3	1830 5.4
26	TH	0136 2.2	0725 5.4	1418 2.2	2002 5.6
27	F	0305 2.0	0841 5.7	1543 1.8	2118 5.9
28	SA	0426 1.6	0943 6.1	1657 1.4	2218 6.3
29	SU	0532 1.2	1032 6.6	1758 1.0	2306 6.6
30	M	0627 1.0	1115 6.8	1850 0.7	○ 2346 6.7
31	TU	0713 0.8	1155 6.9	1935 0.5	

Extracts

Extract 2: Dover Tide Tables – September to December

TIME ZONE (UT)	ENGLAND – DOVER	SPRING & NEAP TIDES
For Summer Time add ONE hour in **non-shaded areas**	**LAT 51°07'N LONG 1°19'E** TIMES AND HEIGHTS OF HIGH AND LOW WATERS	Dates in red are SPRINGS Dates in blue are NEAPS

SEPTEMBER

Day	Time m	Time m	Time m	Time m
1 W	0023 6.7	0752 0.8	1233 7.0	2014 0.6
2 TH	0057 6.6	0826 0.8	1315 6.9	2047 0.7
3 F	0131 6.5	0855 1.0	1346 6.7	2115 0.9
4 SA	0206 6.3	0920 1.2	1422 6.5	2140 1.3
5 SU	0243 6.0	0942 1.5	1458 6.1	2203 1.6
6 M	0325 5.7	1009 1.9	1542 5.7	◐ 2233 2.1
7 TU	0422 5.3	1048 2.3	1645 5.3	2321 2.5
8 W	0536 5.1	1154 2.6	1804 5.0	
9 TH	0101 2.7	0656 5.0	1349 2.6	1927 5.1
10 F	0230 2.5	0813 5.3	1506 2.3	2045 5.4
11 SA	0335 2.1	0910 5.7	1603 1.9	2133 5.7
12 SU	0427 1.8	0949 6.0	1649 1.5	2207 6.1
13 M	0512 1.5	1022 6.3	1732 1.3	2238 6.3
14 TU	0552 1.3	1054 6.5	1812 1.1	● 2310 6.4
15 W	0630 1.2	1126 6.7	1851 1.0	2341 6.5
16 TH	0706 1.1	1157 6.8	1928 0.9	
17 F	0012 6.6	0740 1.1	1230 6.8	2002 0.9
18 SA	0043 6.7	0812 1.1	1304 6.8	2034 1.0
19 SU	0118 6.6	0845 1.2	1341 6.7	2107 1.2
20 M	0158 6.4	0922 1.4	1424 6.4	2146 1.5
21 TU	0246 6.1	1005 1.7	1519 5.9	◐ 2234 1.9
22 W	0352 5.6	1103 2.2	1645 5.5	2345 2.4
23 TH	0542 5.2	1233 2.4	1835 5.3	
24 F	0132 2.4	0719 5.3	1418 2.2	2008 5.6
25 SA	0309 2.1	0836 5.8	1546 1.7	2118 6.0
26 SU	0424 1.6	0932 6.2	1652 1.2	2209 6.4
27 M	0520 1.2	1016 6.6	1745 0.9	2250 6.6
28 TU	0606 1.0	1055 6.8	1830 0.7	○ 2324 6.7
29 W	0647 0.9	1132 7.0	1910 0.6	2356 6.7
30 TH	0721 0.9	1207 7.0	1943 0.7	

OCTOBER

Day	Time m	Time m	Time m	Time m
1 F	0028 6.7	0750 1.0	1242 6.9	2010 0.9
2 SA	0100 6.6	0815 1.1	1315 6.7	2032 1.2
3 SU	0132 6.4	0836 1.3	1345 6.4	2052 1.4
4 M	0203 6.1	0858 1.6	1415 6.1	2115 1.7
5 TU	0235 5.8	0928 1.9	1450 5.7	2148 2.1
6 W	0325 5.4	1008 2.3	1602 5.2	◐ 2232 2.5
7 TH	0455 5.1	1104 2.6	1731 5.0	2348 2.8
8 F	0616 5.0	1302 2.8	1851 5.0	
9 SA	0154 2.7	0731 5.2	1429 2.4	2002 5.3
10 SU	0303 2.3	0828 5.6	1527 1.9	2051 5.7
11 M	0355 1.9	0909 6.0	1604 1.5	2129 6.1
12 TU	0439 1.6	0944 6.3	1658 1.2	2203 6.4
13 W	0520 1.3	1018 6.6	1741 1.0	2236 6.6
14 TH	0600 1.2	1051 6.8	1821 0.9	● 2309 6.7
15 F	0637 1.1	1126 6.9	1859 0.9	2342 6.8
16 SA	0713 1.0	1201 7.0	1936 0.9	
17 SU	0018 6.8	0749 1.0	1239 6.9	2011 1.0
18 M	0057 6.7	0826 1.2	1321 6.7	2048 1.3
19 TU	0142 6.4	0907 1.4	1410 6.3	2130 1.6
20 W	0238 6.0	0955 1.8	1517 5.8	◐ 2224 2.1
21 TH	0357 5.6	1100 2.2	1652 5.4	2344 2.4
22 F	0531 5.4	1236 2.3	1831 5.4	
23 SA	0129 2.4	0703 5.5	1414 2.0	1959 5.6
24 SU	0256 2.0	0816 5.9	1531 1.6	2101 6.0
25 M	0401 1.6	0909 6.3	1631 1.2	2146 6.3
26 TU	0453 1.4	0951 6.6	1720 0.9	2224 6.5
27 W	0536 1.1	1029 6.7	1802 0.8	2256 6.6
28 TH	0614 1.0	1106 6.8	1837 0.9	○ 2327 6.6
29 F	0646 1.0	1141 6.8	1907 1.0	● 2309 6.7
30 SA	0000 6.6	0714 1.1	1215 6.7	1931 1.2
31 SU	0033 6.5	0738 1.3	1246 6.5	1952 1.3

NOVEMBER

Day	Time m	Time m	Time m	Time m
1 M	0104 6.4	0801 1.4	1314 6.3	2014 1.5
2 TU	0133 6.2	0828 1.6	1341 6.0	2043 1.8
3 W	0201 5.9	0902 1.9	1414 5.7	2119 2.1
4 TH	0239 5.6	0943 2.2	1515 5.3	2204 2.4
5 F	0403 5.3	1036 2.5	1653 5.0	◐ 2304 2.7
6 SA	0529 5.1	1202 2.6	1808 5.1	
7 SU	0055 2.7	0638 5.3	1337 2.4	1913 5.3
8 M	0214 2.4	0736 5.6	1439 2.0	2005 5.7
9 TU	0310 2.0	0822 5.9	1531 1.6	2048 6.0
10 W	0359 1.7	0902 6.3	1620 1.3	2125 6.3
11 TH	0444 1.4	0940 6.6	1706 1.1	2202 6.6
12 F	0528 1.2	1018 6.8	1751 0.9	● 2239 6.7
13 SA	0610 1.1	1057 6.9	1834 0.9	2318 6.8
14 SU	0651 1.0	1138 7.0	1915 0.9	
15 M	0000 6.8	0732 1.0	1223 6.8	1955 1.1
16 TU	0046 6.7	0816 1.1	1311 6.6	2039 1.3
17 W	0138 6.5	0903 1.4	1409 6.2	2128 1.6
18 TH	0240 6.1	0959 1.7	1521 5.9	2227 2.0
19 F	0350 5.9	1108 1.9	1643 5.6	◐ 2343 2.2
20 SA	0506 5.7	1227 2.0	1810 5.5	
21 SU	0103 2.2	0627 5.7	1345 1.8	1927 5.6
22 M	0216 2.0	0739 5.9	1455 1.6	2027 5.9
23 TU	0320 1.7	0834 6.1	1555 1.3	2113 6.1
24 W	0414 1.5	0920 6.3	1646 1.2	2152 6.2
25 TH	0500 1.4	1001 6.5	1728 1.2	2227 6.3
26 F	0540 1.3	1040 6.5	1803 1.2	○ 2301 6.4
27 SA	0614 1.3	1116 6.5	1832 1.3	2336 6.5
28 SU	0645 1.3	1151 6.4	1859 1.4	
29 M	0011 6.4	0712 1.4	1225 6.3	1924 1.5
30 TU	0045 6.3	0745 1.5	1256 6.1	1952 1.6

DECEMBER

Day	Time m	Time m	Time m	Time m
1 W	0116 6.2	0811 1.6	1325 5.9	2025 1.7
2 TH	0145 6.0	0847 1.8	1358 5.7	2102 1.9
3 F	0220 5.8	0928 1.9	1442 5.5	2145 2.1
4 SA	0308 5.6	1016 2.1	1547 5.3	2235 2.3
5 SU	0415 5.4	1117 2.2	1708 5.2	◐ 2341 2.4
6 M	0529 5.4	1233 2.2	1817 5.3	
7 TU	0105 2.4	0635 5.6	1343 2.0	1915 5.6
8 W	0214 2.1	0731 5.8	1443 1.7	2004 5.8
9 TH	0313 1.8	0819 6.2	1539 1.4	2049 6.1
10 F	0407 1.6	0905 6.5	1633 1.2	2133 6.4
11 SA	0459 1.3	0951 6.7	1726 1.0	2218 6.6
12 SU	0549 1.1	1038 6.8	1815 1.0	● 2305 6.7
13 M	0638 1.0	1126 6.8	1904 1.0	2353 6.8
14 TU	0727 1.0	1217 6.7	1953 1.0	
15 W	0043 6.7	0818 1.0	1310 6.5	2043 1.2
16 TH	0137 6.6	0911 1.1	1408 6.3	2134 1.4
17 F	0232 6.4	1005 1.3	1510 6.1	2227 1.6
18 SA	0330 6.2	1101 1.4	1615 5.8	◐ 2322 1.8
19 SU	0431 6.0	1159 1.6	1724 5.6	
20 M	0021 1.9	0537 5.8	1259 1.7	1834 5.5
21 TU	0122 2.0	0647 5.8	1400 1.7	1937 5.6
22 W	0225 2.0	0751 5.8	1502 1.7	2032 5.7
23 TH	0326 1.9	0846 5.9	1601 1.6	2119 5.8
24 F	0422 1.7	0935 6.0	1651 1.6	2202 6.0
25 SA	0508 1.6	1019 6.1	1730 1.5	2241 6.2
26 SU	0548 1.5	1058 6.2	1805 1.5	○ 2319 6.3
27 M	0622 1.4	1135 6.2	1836 1.5	2355 6.3
28 TU	0655 1.4	1209 6.2	1908 1.5	
29 W	0029 6.3	0727 1.4	1242 6.1	1940 1.5
30 TH	0100 6.3	0802 1.5	1312 6.0	2015 1.6
31 F	0129 6.2	0839 1.5	1342 5.9	2051 1.7

Extract 3: Tidal Streams, based on HW Dover

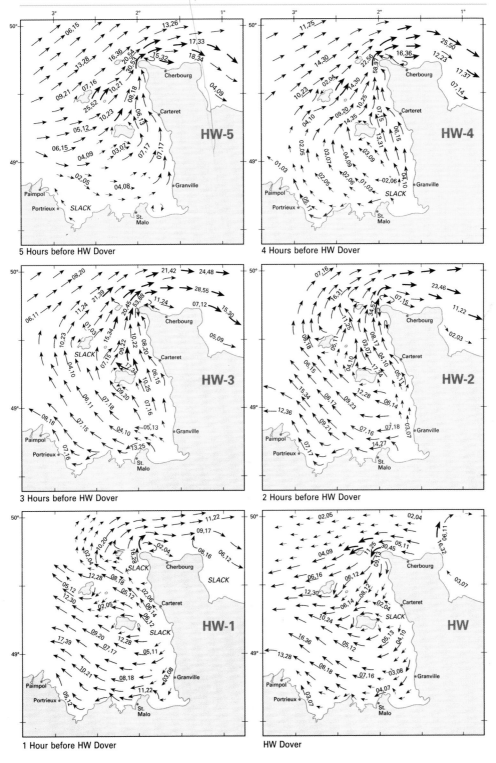

5 Hours before HW Dover

4 Hours before HW Dover

3 Hours before HW Dover

2 Hours before HW Dover

1 Hour before HW Dover

HW Dover

Extracts

Extract 4: Tidal Streams, based on HW Dover (continued)

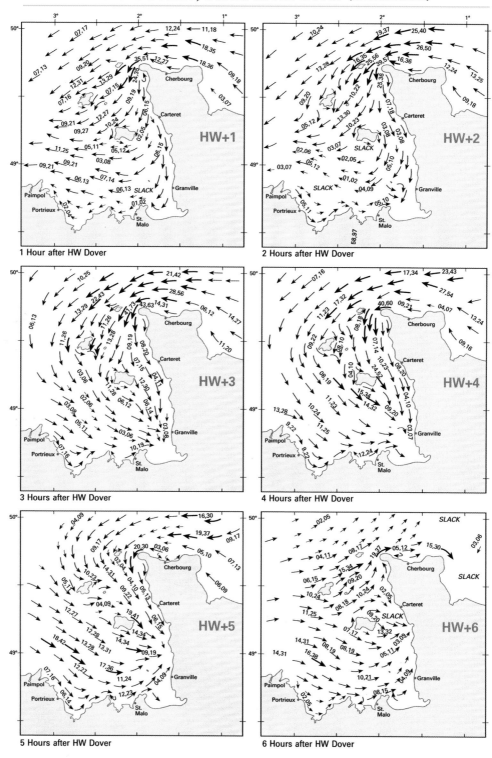

1 Hour after HW Dover

2 Hours after HW Dover

3 Hours after HW Dover

4 Hours after HW Dover

5 Hours after HW Dover

6 Hours after HW Dover

Extract 5: St Helier Tide Table

TIME ZONE (UT)
For Summer Time add ONE hour in **non-shaded areas**

CHANNEL ISLANDS – ST HELIER
LAT 49°11'N LONG 2°07'W
TIMES AND HEIGHTS OF HIGH AND LOW WATERS

SPRING & NEAP TIDES
Dates in red are SPRINGS
Dates in blue are NEAPS

SEPTEMBER

Day	Time	m	Time	m		Day	Time	m	Time	m
1	0222	0.7	0754	11.2		16	0152	1.3	0728	10.9
	W 1437	1.0	2010	11.5			TH 1404	1.3	1940	11.2
2	0258	0.9	0828	11.0		17	0225	1.2	0801	11.0
	TH 1510	1.3	2043	11.1			F 1438	1.3	2014	11.2
3	0329	1.3	0859	10.6		18	0258	1.4	0834	10.8
	F 1539	1.8	2114	10.5			SA 1512	1.6	2049	10.8
4	0355	2.0	0927	10.0		19	0330	1.8	0908	10.4
	SA 1605	2.4	2142	9.7			SU 1546	2.0	2123	10.2
5	0419	2.7	0954	9.4		20	0403	2.4	0942	9.8
	SU 1630	3.1	2210	8.9			M 1623	2.7	2202	9.5
6	0444	3.4	1023	8.7		21	0441	3.1	1023	9.0
	M 1659	3.8	◑ 2244	8.1			TU 1710	3.4	● 2252	8.6
7	0518	4.2	1104	7.9		22	0534	3.9	1125	8.3
	TU 1747	4.5	2341	7.4			W 1821	4.0		
8	0620	4.8	1224	7.3		23	0016	7.9	0704	4.4
	W 1916	4.9					TH 1315	7.9	2007	4.1
9	0153	7.1	0807	4.9		24	0222	7.9	0858	4.1
	TH 1434	7.4	2111	4.6			F 1505	8.5	2144	3.4
10	0330	7.6	0946	4.4		25	0349	8.7	1020	3.3
	F 1549	8.1	2224	3.9			SA 1613	9.4	2252	2.5
11	0425	8.3	1045	3.7		26	0446	9.7	1119	2.3
	SA 1637	8.8	2314	3.1			SU 1705	10.3	2346	1.7
12	0507	9.1	1131	2.9		27	0532	10.4	1208	1.6
	SU 1718	9.6	2357	2.4			M 1749	11.0		
13	0544	9.7	1213	2.3		28	0033	1.1	0613	11.0
	M 1755	10.2					TU 1253	1.2	○ 1829	11.4
14	0037	1.9	0619	10.2		29	0115	0.9	0650	11.2
	TU 1252	1.8	● 1830	10.7			W 1331	1.1	1906	11.5
15	0116	1.5	0654	10.6		30	0151	0.9	0724	11.2
	W 1329	1.5	1905	11.0			TH 1405	1.2	1940	11.3

OCTOBER

Day	Time	m	Time	m		Day	Time	m	Time	m
1	0222	1.2	0755	11.0		16	0159	1.2	0735	11.2
	F 1435	1.5	2010	10.9			SA 1415	1.2	1952	11.3
2	0249	1.6	0823	10.6		17	0234	1.4	0811	11.0
	SA 1501	1.9	2038	10.4			SU 1452	1.5	2029	10.9
3	0313	2.1	0848	10.1		18	0309	1.8	0847	10.6
	SU 1525	2.5	2104	9.7			M 1530	2.0	2108	10.2
4	0336	2.8	0912	9.5		19	0347	2.5	0926	9.9
	M 1549	3.1	2129	8.9			TU 1612	2.7	2153	9.3
5	0400	3.5	0938	8.8		20	0430	3.3	1014	9.1
	TU 1617	3.7	2157	8.1			W 1706	3.4	◑ 2252	8.5
6	0432	4.3	1010	8.1		21	0532	4.1	1126	8.3
	W 1700	4.5	◑ 2244	7.4			TH 1825	4.0		
7	0528	4.9	1115	7.3		22	0026	7.9	0708	4.4
	TH 1824	5.0					F 1317	8.2	2007	3.9
8	0105	7.0	0714	5.2		23	0217	8.2	0850	4.0
	F 1352	7.2	2026	4.8			SA 1450	8.7	2130	3.2
9	0258	7.5	0907	4.7		24	0330	8.9	1001	3.1
	SA 1515	7.9	2148	4.1			SU 1552	9.5	2230	2.4
10	0352	8.3	1011	3.8		25	0422	9.7	1055	2.4
	SU 1604	8.8	2239	3.2			M 1641	10.2	2320	1.8
11	0433	9.1	1057	3.0		26	0506	10.3	1142	1.8
	M 1644	9.6	2322	2.5			TU 1723	10.7		
12	0511	9.8	1140	2.3		27	0004	1.5	0544	10.7
	TU 1723	10.3					W 1223	1.6	1801	10.9
13	0004	1.9	0547	10.4		28	0042	1.4	0620	10.9
	W 1221	1.8	1800	10.8			TH 1259	1.5	○ 1837	11.0
14	0044	1.4	0623	10.9		29	0116	1.5	0655	10.9
	TH 1301	1.4	● 1837	11.2			F 1331	1.6	1910	10.8
15	0123	1.2	0659	11.2		30	0145	1.7	0722	10.8
	F 1339	1.2	1914	11.4			SA 1400	1.8	1940	10.6
						31	0212	2.0	0750	10.5
							SU 1427	2.1	2008	10.1

NOVEMBER

Day	Time	m	Time	m		Day	Time	m	Time	m
1	0238	2.4	0816	10.1		16	0257	1.9	0837	10.7
	M 1453	2.6	2035	9.6			TU 1523	1.9	2104	10.1
2	0305	2.9	0842	9.6		17	0341	2.5	0923	10.0
	TU 1521	3.1	2103	8.9			W 1612	2.5	2155	9.4
3	0332	3.5	0910	9.0		18	0432	3.2	1017	9.4
	W 1552	3.7	2134	8.3			TH 1710	3.1	2257	8.8
4	0406	4.2	0944	8.3		19	0536	3.7	1126	8.8
	TH 1635	4.3	2220	7.6			F 1823	3.5	◑	
5	0458	4.7	1041	7.7		20	0015	8.4	0656	4.0
	F 1744	4.7	◑ 2353	7.2			SA 1251	8.6	1943	3.5
6	0622	5.0	1231	7.4		21	0140	8.4	0817	3.7
	SA 1921	4.7					SU 1411	8.8	2055	3.2
7	0152	7.5	0802	4.7		22	0250	8.8	0925	3.3
	SU 1413	7.8	2049	4.2			M 1515	9.3	2154	2.7
8	0258	8.1	0918	4.0		23	0346	9.4	1021	2.8
	M 1513	8.6	2149	3.4			TU 1608	9.7	2245	2.4
9	0347	8.9	1012	3.2		24	0432	9.8	1109	2.4
	TU 1600	9.3	2239	2.7			W 1653	10.0	2329	2.2
10	0430	9.7	1100	2.5		25	0513	10.1	1151	2.2
	W 1644	10.1	2325	2.1			TH 1733	10.2		
11	0511	10.3	1145	1.9		26	0008	2.1	0549	10.3
	TH 1727	10.7					F 1228	2.1	○ 1810	10.3
12	0009	1.6	0555	10.8		27	0043	2.1	0623	10.4
	F 1230	1.5	● 1809	11.1			SA 1302	2.1	1844	10.2
13	0053	1.4	0632	11.2		28	0114	2.1	0656	10.4
	SA 1313	1.3	1851	11.2			SU 1333	2.2	1917	10.1
14	0134	1.3	0712	11.3		29	0145	2.3	0726	10.3
	SU 1355	1.3	1934	11.1			M 1404	2.3	1949	9.8
15	0215	1.5	0754	11.1		30	0216	2.5	0757	10.0
	M 1438	1.5	2018	10.7			TU 1435	2.6	2020	9.5

DECEMBER

Day	Time	m	Time	m		Day	Time	m	Time	m
1	0246	2.9	0827	9.6		16	0342	2.1	0923	10.5
	W 1506	3.0	2052	9.1			TH 1614	2.0	2154	9.9
2	0318	3.3	0859	9.2		17	0432	2.6	1013	10.0
	TH 1540	3.4	2127	8.6			F 1706	2.4	2245	9.4
3	0354	3.7	0936	8.8		18	0525	3.0	1107	9.5
	F 1621	3.8	2210	8.2			SA 1801	2.9	◑ 2342	8.9
4	0439	4.1	1024	8.3		19	0624	3.4	1208	9.0
	SA 1713	4.1	2308	7.9			SU 1901	3.2		
5	0538	4.4	1130	8.0		20	0045	8.6	0728	3.6
	SU 1820	4.2	◑				M 1316	8.7	2003	3.4
6	0025	7.8	0652	4.4		21	0153	8.5	0834	3.6
	M 1250	8.0	1936	4.1			TU 1424	8.7	2105	3.3
7	0144	8.1	0810	4.1		22	0257	8.7	0937	3.4
	TU 1405	8.4	2048	3.7			W 1526	8.8	2203	3.2
8	0248	8.6	0918	3.5		23	0354	9.0	1033	3.2
	W 1507	9.0	2150	3.1			TH 1621	9.1	2254	3.0
9	0343	9.3	1017	2.9		24	0442	9.3	1122	2.9
	TH 1603	9.6	2245	2.5			F 1708	9.3	2339	2.8
10	0434	9.9	1111	2.3		25	0525	9.6	1204	2.7
	F 1655	10.2	2337	2.0			SA 1750	9.5		
11	0523	10.5	1203	1.8		26	0018	2.6	0603	9.9
	SA 1746	10.6					SU 1242	2.5	○ 1828	9.7
12	0028	1.7	0611	10.9		27	0056	2.5	0639	10.0
	SU 1254	1.4	● 1836	10.9			M 1318	2.4	1905	9.8
13	0117	1.5	0658	11.1		28	0130	2.5	0713	10.0
	M 1344	1.3	1926	10.9			TU 1352	2.4	1939	9.7
14	0206	1.6	0746	11.1		29	0204	2.5	0747	10.0
	TU 1433	1.3	2015	10.8			W 1426	2.4	2012	9.6
15	0254	1.8	0834	10.9		30	0237	2.6	0819	9.9
	W 1523	1.6	2104	10.4			TH 1459	2.6	2045	9.5
						31	0309	2.8	0853	9.7
							F 1532	2.8	2118	9.2

Chart Datum: 5·88 metres below Ordnance Datum (Local)

Extracts

Extract 6: Port Information for St Helier

ST HELIER

Standard Port ST HELIER

Times				Height (metres)			
High Water		Low Water		MHWS	MHWN	MLWN	MLWS
0300	0900	0200	0900	11·0	8·1	4·0	1·4
1500	2100	1400	2100				
Differences ST CATHERINE BAY							
0000	+0010	+0010	+0010	0·0	−0·1	0·0	+0·1
Differences BRAYE							
+0050	+0040	+0025	+0105	−4·8	−3·4	−1·5	−0·5

Jersey (Channel Is) 49°10'·57N 02°06'·98W ✲✲✲🚤🚤 ✩✩

CHARTS AC *3655, 1137, 3278, 5604*; SHOM 7160, 7161, 6938; ECM 534, 1014; Imray C33B; Stanfords 16, 26

TIDES −0455 Dover; ML 6·1; Duration 0545; Zone 0 (UT)
NOTE: St Helier is a Standard Port. The tidal range is very large.

SHELTER Excellent. Visitors berth in **St Helier marina**, access HW±3 over sill (CD+3·6m); hinged gate rises 1·4m above sill to retain 5m. Digital gauge shows depth over sill. A waiting pontoon is to W of marina ent, near LB. Depths in marina vary from 2·8m at ent to 2·1m at N end. 🚫 berths as directed by staff (yachts >12m LOA or >2·1m draft, use pontoon A). Good shelter in **La Collette basin**, 1·8m; access H24, to await the tide. Caution: Ent narrow at LWS; keep close to W side; PHM buoys mark shoal on E side. Waiting berths on pontoon D and W side of C. FVs berth on W of basin. **Elizabeth marina** is mainly for local boats; access HW±3 over sill/flap gate; max LOA 20m, drafts 2·1 – 3·5m. No ⚓ in St Helier Rds due to shipping & fish storage boxes.

NAVIGATION WPT 49°09'·95N 02°07'·38W, 023°/0·74M to front ldg lt. This WPT is common to all St Helier appr's:
1. W Passage (082°); beware race off Noirmont Pt, HW to HW +4.
1A. NW Passage (095°, much used by yachts) passes 6ca S of La Corbière lt ho to join W Passage abm Noirmont Pt.

LIGHTS AND MARKS Power stn chy (95m, floodlit) and W concave roofs of Fort Regent are conspic, close E of R & G ldg line. **W Passage** ldg lts: Front Oc 5s 23m 14M; rear Oc R 5s 46m 12M and Dog's Nest bn (unlit) lead 082°, N of Les Fours, NCM Q, and Ruaudière, SHM Fl G 3s, buoys, to a position close to E Rock, SHM buoy QG, where course is altered to pick up the **Red & Green Passage** ldg lts 023°: Front Oc G 5s; rear Oc R 5s, synch; (now easier to see against town lts) Daymarks are red dayglow patches on front dolphin and rear lt twr. Nos 2 and 4 PHM buoys mark the fairway N of Platte Rk (Fl R 1·5s). Outer pier hds and dolphin are painted white and floodlit. Inner ldg lts 078°, both FG on W columns are not essential for yachts.

IPTS (Sigs 1-4) are shown from the base of the Port Control tower and are easily seen from Small Road, La Collette and the Main Hbr. Repeater lts are shown in conjunction from the top of the tower, during shipping and high-speed ferry movements. They are: L Fl R 5s with Sig 1; Oc R 8s with Sig 2; Oc G 8s with Sig 3; and Oc Y 4s with Sig 4. The Oc Y 4s is used whenever possible. It exempts power-driven craft <25m LOA from the main display signals. Keep to stbd, well clear of shipping, and keep a sharp all-round lookout. Monitor VHF Ch 14 during arr/dep.
Local IPTS control arr/dep to/from St Helier and Elizabeth marinas (but not La Collette), with large digital tide gauges showing depth over the sills.

R/T Monitor *St Helier Port Control* VHF Ch 14 (H24) for ferry/ shipping movements. No marina VHF, but call *Port Control* if essential. Do not use Ch M. If unable to pass messages to *Port Control*, these can be relayed via *Jersey Radio* CRS, Ch **82** 25 16 (H24) or ☎ 741121.

St Helier Pierheads broadcasts recorded wind info every 2 mins on VHF Ch 18. It consists of: wind direction, speed and gusts meaned over the last 2 minutes.

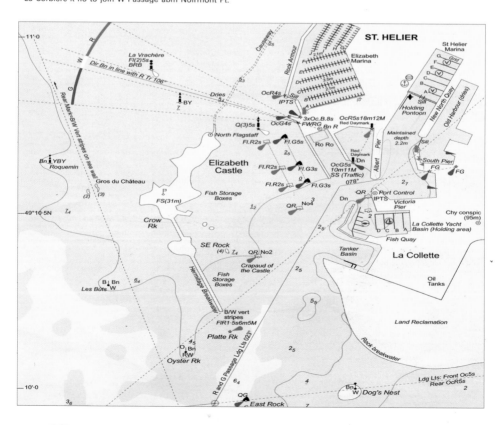

Extract 7: St Helier Tidal Curve

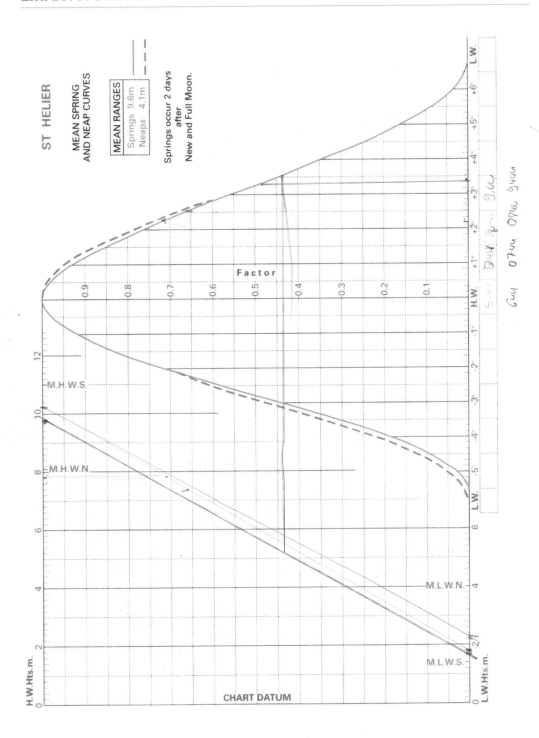

ST HELIER

MEAN SPRING
AND NEAP CURVES

MEAN RANGES
Springs 9.6m
Neaps 4.1m

Springs occur 2 days
after
New and Full Moon.

Extracts

Extract 8: Cherbourg Tidal Curve

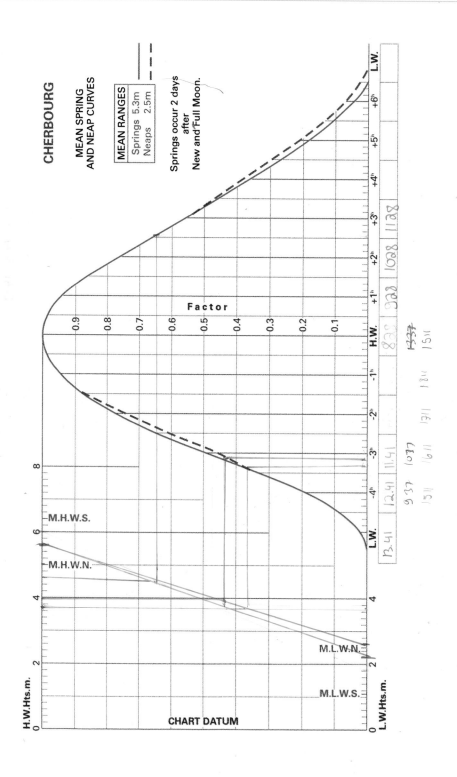

CHERBOURG

MEAN SPRING
AND NEAP CURVES

MEAN RANGES
Springs 5.3m
Neaps 2.5m

Springs occur 2 days
after
New and Full Moon.

Extract 9: Cherbourg Tide Table

TIME ZONE -0100
(French Standard Time)
Subtract 1 hour for UT
For French Summer Time add
ONE hour in **non-shaded areas**

FRANCE – CHERBOURG
LAT 49°39′N   LONG 1°38′W
TIMES AND HEIGHTS OF HIGH AND LOW WATERS

SPRING & NEAP TIDES
Dates in red are SPRINGS
Dates in blue are NEAPS

SEPTEMBER

Time m	Time m
1 0447 0.7 / 1025 6.4 / W 1703 1.0 / 2237 6.7	**16** 0421 1.0 / 0958 6.3 / TH 1633 1.1 / 2207 6.5
2 0522 0.9 / 1059 6.3 / TH 1737 1.2 / 2312 6.4	**17** 0454 1.0 / 1030 6.3 / F 1707 1.1 / 2241 6.4
3 0555 1.1 / 1129 6.1 / F 1810 1.5 / 2344 6.1	**18** 0527 1.1 / 1103 6.3 / SA 1742 1.3 / 2315 6.3
4 0625 1.5 / 1157 5.8 / SA 1841 1.8	**19** 0601 1.3 / 1135 6.1 / SU 1818 1.5 / 2351 6.0
5 0013 5.7 / 0654 2.0 / SU 1225 5.5 / 1914 2.2	**20** 0639 1.7 / 1211 5.8 / M 1900 1.9
6 0045 5.3 / 0727 2.4 / M 1258 5.1 / ◑ 1955 2.6	**21** 0033 5.6 / 0723 2.2 / TU 1257 5.4 / ◐ 1954 2.3
7 0126 4.8 / 0811 2.9 / TU 1345 4.8 / 2057 3.0	**22** 0132 5.1 / 0825 2.6 / W 1405 5.1 / 2112 2.6
8 0242 4.4 / 0927 3.2 / W 1524 4.5 / 2243 3.1	**23** 0309 4.8 / 1001 2.9 / TH 1556 4.9 / 2258 2.6
9 0456 4.4 / 1126 3.2 / TH 1723 4.6	**24** 0508 4.9 / 1147 2.7 / F 1733 5.2
10 0020 2.8 / 0615 4.8 / F 1244 2.8 / 1826 5.0	**25** 0029 2.1 / 0625 5.4 / SA 1300 2.2 / 1839 5.7
11 0117 2.4 / 0702 5.2 / SA 1335 2.4 / 1910 5.4	**26** 0130 1.6 / 0719 5.8 / SU 1355 1.7 / 1931 6.1
12 0200 2.0 / 0740 5.5 / SU 1417 2.0 / 1949 5.8	**27** 0220 1.2 / 0804 6.2 / M 1441 1.4 / 2016 6.5
13 0238 1.6 / 0816 5.8 / M 1451 1.7 / 2025 6.1	**28** 0304 1.0 / 0844 6.4 / TU 1522 1.1 / ○ 2056 6.7
14 0313 1.3 / 0851 6.1 / TU 1525 1.4 / ● 2100 6.3	**29** 0342 0.9 / 0920 6.5 / W 1559 1.1 / 2133 6.7
15 0347 1.1 / 0925 6.2 / W 1559 1.2 / 2134 6.4	**30** 0417 0.9 / 0953 6.5 / TH 1633 1.1 / 2207 6.6

OCTOBER

Time m	Time m
1 0448 1.1 / 1023 6.3 / F 1704 1.3 / 2238 6.3	**16** 0427 1.0 / 1002 6.5 / SA 1643 1.0 / 2217 6.5
2 0518 1.3 / 1050 6.2 / SA 1734 1.5 / 2307 6.0	**17** 0503 1.1 / 1037 6.4 / SU 1721 1.2 / 2256 6.3
3 0546 1.7 / 1116 5.9 / SU 1803 1.9 / 2335 5.7	**18** 0541 1.4 / 1114 6.2 / M 1802 1.5 / 2337 6.0
4 0614 2.1 / 1141 5.6 / M 1833 2.2	**19** 0622 1.8 / 1155 5.9 / TU 1848 1.9
5 0003 5.2 / 0645 2.5 / TU 1211 5.2 / 1910 2.6	**20** 0026 5.5 / 0713 2.3 / W 1248 5.5 / ◐ 1948 2.3
6 0041 4.8 / 0725 3.0 / W 1254 4.8 / ◑ 2003 3.0	**21** 0134 5.1 / 0824 2.8 / TH 1404 5.1 / 2113 2.5
7 0149 4.5 / 0833 3.3 / TH 1418 4.5 / 2144 3.2	**22** 0321 4.9 / 1008 2.9 / F 1554 5.0 / 2255 2.4
8 0418 4.4 / 1042 3.3 / F 1640 4.6 / 2337 2.9	**23** 0503 5.1 / 1140 2.6 / SA 1719 5.3
9 0541 4.7 / 1209 3.0 / SA 1749 4.9	**24** 0013 2.1 / 0607 5.5 / SU 1243 2.2 / 1818 5.7
10 0040 2.5 / 0627 5.1 / SU 1259 2.5 / 1834 5.3	**25** 0110 1.7 / 0655 5.8 / M 1334 1.8 / 1907 6.1
11 0123 2.0 / 0705 5.6 / M 1339 2.1 / 1913 5.8	**26** 0156 1.4 / 0737 6.1 / TU 1417 1.5 / 1950 6.3
12 0201 1.6 / 0742 5.9 / TU 1416 1.7 / 1951 6.1	**27** 0236 1.2 / 0814 6.3 / W 1456 1.3 / 2029 6.4
13 0238 1.3 / 0817 6.2 / W 1453 1.4 / 2028 6.4	**28** 0313 1.2 / 0849 6.4 / TH 1531 1.3 / ○ 2104 6.4
14 0314 1.1 / 0852 6.4 / TH 1530 1.1 / ● 2104 6.5	**29** 0345 1.2 / 0920 6.3 / F 1604 1.3 / 2137 6.3
15 0351 0.9 / 0927 6.5 / F 1606 1.0 / 2140 6.6	**30** 0416 1.4 / 0948 6.3 / SA 1635 1.4 / 2207 6.1
	31 0446 1.6 / 1016 6.1 / SU 1705 1.6 / 2237 5.9

NOVEMBER

Time m	Time m
1 0515 1.9 / 1043 5.9 / M 1735 1.9 / 2306 5.6	**16** 0529 1.5 / 1102 6.3 / TU 1754 1.4 / 2333 6.0
2 0545 2.2 / 1111 5.6 / TU 1806 2.2 / 2338 5.3	**17** 0617 1.9 / 1150 6.0 / W 1847 1.7
3 0618 2.6 / 1144 5.3 / W 1843 2.5	**18** 0027 5.6 / 0714 2.3 / TH 1247 5.6 / 1949 2.1
4 0018 4.9 / 0658 2.9 / TH 1228 5.0 / 1931 2.8	**19** 0136 5.2 / 0825 2.6 / F 1401 5.3 / ◑ 2106 2.3
5 0119 4.6 / 0758 3.2 / F 1337 4.7 / ◑ 2047 3.0	**20** 0305 5.1 / 0951 2.7 / SA 1527 5.2 / 2228 2.3
6 0304 4.5 / 0933 3.3 / SA 1523 4.6 / 2227 2.9	**21** 0427 5.2 / 1109 2.5 / SU 1643 5.3 / 2337 2.1
7 0438 4.7 / 1106 3.0 / SU 1647 4.9 / 2340 2.6	**22** 0530 5.4 / 1211 2.3 / M 1743 5.6
8 0535 5.1 / 1207 2.6 / M 1742 5.2	**23** 0036 1.9 / 0620 5.7 / TU 1303 2.0 / 1835 5.8
9 0034 2.2 / 0619 5.5 / TU 1254 2.2 / 1828 5.6	**24** 0124 1.7 / 0704 5.9 / W 1349 1.8 / 1920 6.0
10 0118 1.8 / 0700 5.9 / W 1337 1.8 / 1911 6.0	**25** 0206 1.6 / 0743 6.0 / TH 1429 1.6 / 2001 6.0
11 0200 1.4 / 0739 6.2 / TH 1419 1.4 / 1953 6.3	**26** 0243 1.6 / 0818 6.1 / F 1506 1.6 / ○ 2038 6.1
12 0241 1.2 / 0818 6.4 / F 1501 1.2 / ● 2035 6.5	**27** 0318 1.6 / 0852 6.1 / SA 1540 1.6 / 2113 6.0
13 0322 1.1 / 0857 6.6 / SA 1542 1.0 / 2117 6.5	**28** 0351 1.7 / 0923 6.1 / SU 1613 1.6 / 2146 5.9
14 0403 1.1 / 0937 6.6 / SU 1624 1.0 / 2200 6.5	**29** 0424 1.8 / 0953 6.0 / M 1645 1.7 / 2218 5.8
15 0445 1.2 / 1018 6.5 / M 1708 1.1 / 2245 6.3	**30** 0456 2.0 / 1024 5.9 / TU 1718 1.9 / 2250 5.6

DECEMBER

Time m	Time m
1 0528 2.2 / 1056 5.7 / W 1751 2.1 / 2325 5.4	**16** 0616 1.7 / 1148 6.2 / TH 1844 1.4
2 0603 2.4 / 1132 5.5 / TH 1828 2.3	**17** 0025 5.8 / 0710 2.0 / F 1242 5.9 / 1940 1.7
3 0005 5.1 / 0643 2.7 / F 1214 5.2 / 1911 2.5	**18** 0122 5.5 / 0809 2.2 / SA 1340 5.6 / ◐ 2039 2.0
4 0056 4.9 / 0733 2.8 / SA 1307 5.0 / 2006 2.6	**19** 0224 5.3 / 0912 2.4 / SU 1444 5.4 / 2142 2.2
5 0201 4.8 / 0837 2.9 / SU 1415 4.9 / ◑ 2114 2.7	**20** 0330 5.2 / 1020 2.5 / M 1550 5.3 / 2248 2.3
6 0316 4.8 / 0951 2.9 / M 1529 4.9 / 2227 2.6	**21** 0435 5.2 / 1126 2.5 / TU 1656 5.2 / 2350 2.3
7 0425 5.0 / 1102 2.7 / TU 1637 5.1 / 2332 2.3	**22** 0535 5.3 / 1226 2.3 / W 1758 5.3
8 0522 5.3 / 1203 2.3 / W 1736 5.4	**23** 0047 2.2 / 0628 5.5 / TH 1319 2.2 / 1852 5.5
9 0031 2.0 / 0613 5.7 / TH 1257 2.0 / 1830 5.7	**24** 0137 2.1 / 0714 5.7 / F 1405 2.0 / 1939 5.6
10 0123 1.7 / 0701 6.0 / F 1348 1.6 / 1921 6.0	**25** 0220 2.0 / 0756 5.8 / SA 1446 1.9 / 2021 5.7
11 0212 1.4 / 0748 6.3 / SA 1437 1.3 / 2011 6.3	**26** 0259 2.0 / 0833 5.9 / SU 1523 1.7 / 2059 5.8
12 0300 1.3 / 0834 6.5 / SU 1525 1.1 / ● 2101 6.4	**27** 0336 1.9 / 0908 5.9 / M 1559 1.7 / 2134 5.8
13 0348 1.2 / 0920 6.6 / M 1613 1.0 / 2150 6.4	**28** 0411 1.9 / 0940 6.0 / TU 1633 1.7 / 2207 5.8
14 0436 1.3 / 1008 6.5 / TU 1702 1.0 / 2240 6.3	**29** 0445 1.9 / 1013 5.9 / W 1707 1.7 / 2240 5.7
15 0525 1.5 / 1057 6.4 / W 1752 1.2 / 2332 6.1	**30** 0518 2.0 / 1046 5.9 / TH 1741 1.8 / 2314 5.6
	31 0552 2.1 / 1122 5.7 / F 1815 1.9 / 2351 5.5

Extracts

Extract 10: St Malo Tide Table

<table>
<tr><td colspan="2">TIME ZONE -0100
(French Standard Time)
Subtract 1 hour for UT
For French Summer Time add
ONE hour in non-shaded areas</td><td colspan="4" align="center">FRANCE – ST MALO
LAT 48°38'N   LONG 2°02'W
TIMES AND HEIGHTS OF HIGH AND LOW WATERS</td><td colspan="2">SPRING & NEAP TIDES
Dates in red are SPRINGS
Dates in blue are NEAPS</td></tr>
</table>

MAY		JUNE		JULY		AUGUST	
Time m	Time m	Time m	Time m	Time m	Time m	Time m	Time m
1 0413 9.7 1103 3.5 SA 1650 10.0 2326 3.3	**16** 0517 10.8 1205 2.7 SU 1740 10.9	**1** 0514 11.1 1210 2.3 TU 1744 11.4	**16** 0031 3.1 0608 10.5 W 1247 3.0 1823 10.9	**1** 0007 2.5 0544 11.1 TH 1304 2.3 1813 11.5	**16** 0048 3.3 0629 10.3 F 1304 3.2 1842 10.7	**1** 0200 1.6 0732 11.8 SU 1424 1.7 1951 12.4	**16** 0157 2.5 0730 11.1 M 1412 2.5 ● 1940 11.6
2 0505 10.6 1158 2.6 SU 1736 10.9	**17** 0029 2.7 0600 11.1 M 1247 2.5 1818 11.2	**2** 0037 2.1 0606 11.7 W 1304 1.8 1833 11.9	**17** 0111 2.9 0647 10.7 TH 1325 2.9 ● 1859 11.1	**2** 0109 2.0 0642 11.5 F 1336 2.0 ○ 1907 12.0	**17** 0130 3.0 0709 10.6 SA 1345 3.0 ● 1919 11.0	**2** 0254 1.2 0820 12.1 M 1514 1.4 2037 12.6	**17** 0236 2.2 0805 11.4 TU 1450 2.2 2015 11.8
3 0021 2.4 0553 11.4 M 1248 1.9 1820 11.6	**18** 0108 2.5 0637 11.3 TU 1324 2.3 1852 11.4	**3** 0130 1.6 0656 12.1 TH 1354 1.5 ○ 1920 12.3	**18** 0147 2.8 0723 10.8 F 1401 2.8 1933 11.2	**3** 0206 1.6 0737 11.8 SA 1430 1.7 1958 12.2	**18** 0209 2.8 0746 10.8 SU 1424 2.8 1955 11.2	**3** 0341 1.1 0903 12.2 TU 1558 1.4 2119 12.5	**18** 0313 1.9 0839 11.6 W 1526 2.0 2049 12.0
4 0111 1.7 0638 12.1 TU 1336 1.4 ○ 1902 12.2	**19** 0143 2.3 0712 11.3 W 1356 2.3 ● 1924 11.5	**4** 0221 1.3 0746 12.2 F 1442 1.5 2006 12.4	**19** 0222 2.7 0757 10.8 SA 1435 2.8 2006 11.2	**4** 0300 1.4 0829 12.0 SU 1521 1.7 2047 12.3	**19** 0247 2.6 0821 10.9 M 1501 2.7 2030 11.3	**4** 0423 1.2 0943 12.0 W 1638 1.7 2158 12.2	**19** 0348 1.8 0912 11.6 TH 1600 2.0 2122 11.9
5 0158 1.3 0721 12.5 W 1421 1.1 1943 12.5	**20** 0215 2.3 0745 11.3 TH 1427 2.3 1955 11.5	**5** 0309 1.3 0834 12.1 SA 1528 1.7 2053 12.3	**20** 0257 2.7 0831 10.8 SU 1509 2.9 2040 11.1	**5** 0351 1.4 0917 11.9 M 1609 1.8 2134 12.1	**20** 0325 2.4 0856 11.0 TU 1538 2.6 2104 11.4	**5** 0500 1.6 1020 11.6 TH 1713 2.2 2235 11.6	**20** 0422 1.9 0944 11.5 F 1634 2.2 2155 11.7
6 0243 1.0 0804 12.7 TH 1503 1.1 2023 12.6	**21** 0245 2.4 0815 11.2 F 1456 2.5 2024 11.4	**6** 0356 1.5 0922 11.8 SU 1614 2.1 2140 11.9	**21** 0331 2.8 0905 10.6 M 1544 3.0 2114 10.9	**6** 0438 1.6 1003 11.6 TU 1654 2.2 2220 11.7	**21** 0401 2.4 0930 11.0 W 1614 2.6 2139 11.3	**6** 0533 2.3 1055 11.0 F 1745 2.9 2310 10.8	**21** 0454 2.2 1017 11.2 SA 1707 2.6 2229 11.2
7 0325 1.1 0846 12.5 F 1543 1.4 2104 12.4	**22** 0314 2.5 0845 10.9 SA 1525 2.8 2054 11.1	**7** 0442 2.0 1011 11.3 M 1702 2.7 2230 11.3	**22** 0407 3.0 0941 10.4 TU 1620 3.3 2151 10.6	**7** 0522 2.0 1047 11.1 W 1738 2.7 2304 11.2	**22** 0437 2.5 1005 10.8 TH 1650 2.8 2215 11.0	**7** 0603 3.0 1129 10.3 SA 1817 3.6 ◑ 2348 10.0	**22** 0526 2.7 1051 10.7 SU 1743 3.1 2307 10.6
8 0405 1.5 0928 12.0 SA 1622 2.0 2146 11.8	**23** 0344 2.8 0915 10.6 SU 1555 3.2 2124 10.7	**8** 0531 2.5 1102 10.7 TU 1750 3.3 2324 10.7	**23** 0444 3.2 1019 10.1 W 1659 3.6 2231 10.3	**8** 0604 2.6 1130 10.6 TH 1821 3.2 2350 10.6	**23** 0513 2.7 1041 10.5 F 1727 3.1 2254 10.7	**8** 0635 3.7 1207 9.7 SU 1856 4.3	**23** 0602 3.3 1132 10.1 M 1826 3.7 ◑ 2355 9.9
9 0447 2.1 1014 11.3 SU 1703 2.8 2233 11.1	**24** 0414 3.2 0948 10.1 M 1627 3.7 2158 10.2	**9** 0623 3.1 1157 10.1 W 1846 3.8 ◑	**24** 0525 3.5 1101 9.8 TH 1743 3.9 2316 10.0	**9** 0646 3.2 1215 10.0 F 1906 3.8 ◑	**24** 0551 3.1 1120 10.2 SA 1808 3.4 2336 10.3	**9** 0035 9.2 0719 4.4 M 1300 9.1 1953 4.8	**24** 0651 4.0 1229 9.5 TU 1928 4.3
10 0532 2.6 1106 10.4 M 1752 3.6 2329 10.2	**25** 0448 3.7 1026 9.6 TU 1704 4.2 2239 9.7	**10** 0025 10.1 0720 3.6 TH 1259 9.6 1949 4.1	**25** 0611 3.7 1150 9.8 F 1834 4.1 ◐	**10** 0041 9.9 0731 3.7 SA 1307 9.6 1958 4.2	**25** 0633 3.4 1206 9.8 SU 1857 3.8 ◐	**10** 0145 8.7 0824 4.9 TU 1422 8.7 2116 5.0	**25** 0112 9.3 0803 4.4 W 1401 9.2 2058 4.4
11 0628 3.6 1211 9.6 TU 1856 4.3 ◑	**26** 0530 4.1 1114 9.1 W 1753 4.6 2334 9.2	**11** 0132 9.8 0823 3.8 F 1408 9.5 2055 4.1	**26** 0010 9.7 0705 3.9 SA 1248 9.3 1935 4.1	**11** 0139 9.5 0824 4.1 SU 1410 9.3 2100 4.4	**26** 0031 9.9 0726 3.8 M 1307 9.5 2000 4.0	**11** 0318 8.6 0950 4.9 W 1554 8.9 2237 4.7	**26** 0257 9.2 0944 4.4 TH 1546 9.5 2232 3.9
12 0047 9.6 0741 4.1 W 1335 9.2 2022 4.5	**27** 0626 4.4 1220 8.8 TH 1859 4.8 ◐	**12** 0241 9.7 0926 3.8 SA 1515 9.6 2158 3.9	**27** 0115 9.6 0809 3.9 SU 1357 9.4 2044 4.0	**12** 0248 9.2 0927 4.3 M 1520 9.3 2206 4.3	**27** 0142 9.6 0836 4.0 TU 1425 9.5 2119 4.0	**12** 0436 9.0 1105 4.5 TH 1659 9.5 2340 4.1	**27** 0430 9.7 1113 3.7 F 1704 10.3 2348 3.0
13 0215 9.5 0906 4.0 TH 1500 9.4 2143 4.2	**28** 0050 9.0 0740 4.5 F 1342 8.8 2020 4.7	**13** 0343 9.8 1025 3.7 SU 1612 9.9 2255 3.6	**28** 0226 9.8 0920 3.7 M 1507 9.7 2155 3.6	**13** 0356 9.3 1031 4.2 TU 1625 9.6 2307 4.0	**28** 0305 9.6 0958 3.8 W 1549 9.8 2239 3.5	**13** 0530 9.6 1202 3.9 F 1746 10.1	**28** 0539 10.6 1224 2.9 SA 1803 11.3
14 0331 9.8 1018 3.6 F 1606 9.9 2249 3.6	**29** 0209 9.2 0901 4.2 SA 1456 9.2 2135 4.1	**14** 0438 10.1 1118 3.4 M 1702 10.3 2345 3.3	**29** 0335 10.1 1031 3.3 TU 1614 10.3 2302 3.1	**14** 0456 9.5 1129 3.9 W 1718 10.0	**29** 0426 10.0 1116 3.4 TH 1704 10.5 2351 2.8	**14** 0032 3.5 0614 10.2 SA 1250 3.4 1827 10.7	**29** 0057 2.1 0633 11.4 SU 1323 2.1 1853 12.1
15 0429 10.3 1117 3.1 SA 1657 10.4 2342 3.1	**30** 0318 9.8 1011 3.6 SU 1559 9.9 2239 3.4	**15** 0526 10.3 1205 3.2 TU 1745 10.6	**30** 0442 10.6 1137 2.8 W 1716 10.9	**15** 0000 3.6 0546 9.9 TH 1220 3.5 1803 10.4	**30** 0538 10.6 1226 2.7 F 1807 11.2	**15** 0116 2.9 0653 10.7 SU 1333 2.9 1904 11.2	**30** 0152 1.4 0720 12.0 M 1413 1.5 ○ 1937 12.6
	31 0419 10.4 1113 2.9 M 1653 10.6 2338 2.7				**31** 0100 2.2 0639 11.3 SA 1328 2.2 ○ 1902 11.9		**31** 0239 1.0 0802 12.4 TU 1458 1.2 2018 12.8

Extract 11: St Malo Tidal Curve

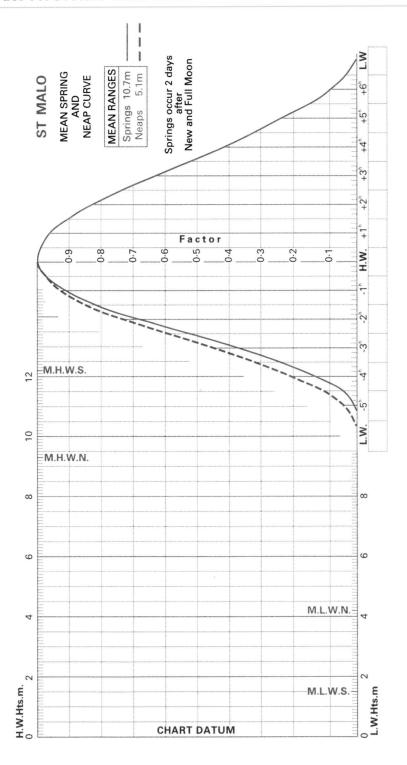

ST MALO

MEAN SPRING
AND
NEAP CURVE

MEAN RANGES
Springs 10.7m
Neaps 5.1m

Springs occur 2 days
after
New and Full Moon

Factor

M.H.W.S.

M.H.W.N.

M.L.W.N.

M.L.W.S.

CHART DATUM

H.W.Hts.m.

L.W.Hts.m

Extract 12: Port Information – St Malo

ST MALO

SHELTER Two options: 1. Lock into Bassin Vauban, min depth 6m. Excellent shelter near the walled city. Berth on pontoon marked for your LOA; no fingers; no turning room. Bassin Duguay-Trouin, beyond bridge, is better for long stay. No ⚓ in basins; 3kn speed limit. Outside the lock 3 waiting buoys are N of appr chan; keep clear of vedette and Condor berths.
Lock operates five times in each direction, ie
Inbound: HW $-2\frac{1}{2}$, $-1\frac{1}{2}$, $-\frac{1}{2}$, HW$+\frac{1}{2}$, $+1\frac{1}{2}$.
Outbound: HW -2, -1, HW, $+1$, $+2$.
Assistance is given with warp-handling; pas de problème.
Lock sigs are IPTS Nos 2, 3 and 5. In addition:
⬤ next to the top lt means both lock gates are open; main message is the same, but beware current. Freeflow operation is rare due to busy road traffic over rolling bridge.
⬤ ⬤ over ⬤ = all movements prohib, except big ship departure.
2. Good shelter nearer St Servan in Bas Sablons marina, entered over sill 2m above CD. Two W waiting buoys outside. Depth of water over sill is shown on a digital gauge atop the bkwtr, visible only from seaward; inside, a conventional gauge at base of bkwtr shows depths <3m. Ⓥ berths are 32-66 (E side) and 43-75 (W side) of pontoon A, and 92-102 and 91-101 on pontoon B. N end of both pontoons are exposed to fresh NW winds.
At **Dinard** there is a yacht ⚓ and moorings, reached by a beaconed chan, all dredged 2m, but virtually full of local boats.

NAVIGATION WPT 48°41'·38N 02°07'·28W [SWM buoy, Iso 4s Whis], 127°/1·9M to Grand Jardin lt, where in fresh W'lies it can be quite rough. Care is needed due to many dangerous rks around the appr chans, plus strong tidal streams. The 3 main chans (see also 9.18.4) are:
1. Petite Porte (130°/129°); best from N or NW and at night.
2. Grande Porte (089°/129°); from the W and at night.
These 2 chans meet at Le Grand Jardin lt and continue 129°.
3. La Grande Conchée (181·5°); most direct from N, but unlit.

LIGHTS AND MARKS See chartlets and 9.18.4.

R/T *St Malo Port* Ch **12** 16 (H24). Marinas Ch 09.

TELEPHONE
ST MALO: Port HM 02·99·20·63·01, fax 02·99·56·48·71; HM (Vauban) 02·99·56·51·91; HM (Bas Sablons) 02·99·81·71·34; Aff Mar 02·99·56·87·00; CROSS 02·98·89·31·31; SNSM 02·98·89·31·31; ⊖ 02·99·81·65·90; Météo 02·99·46·10·46; Auto 08.92.68.08.35; Police 02·99·81·52·30; Ⓗ 02·99·56·56·19; Brit Consul 02·99·46·26·64.

FACILITIES
ST MALO: **Bassin Vauban** (250 + 100 Ⓥ) ☎ 02·99·56·51·91, 📠 02.99.56.57.81, €2.67, C (1 ton); **Société Nautique de la Baie de St. Malo** ☎ 02·99·40·84·42, 📠 02.99.56.39.41, Bar (Ⓥ welcome).
ST SERVAN: **Marina Les Bas-Sablons** (1216 + 64 Ⓥ on pontoon

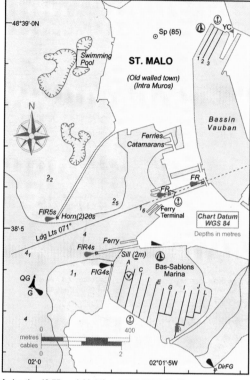

A, berths 43-75 and 32-64) ☎ 02·99·81·71·34, 📠 02.99.81.91.81, €2.22, Slip, C, BH (10 ton), Gaz, R, YC, Bar, P & D pontoon 'I'; Note: Pumps are operated by French credit card; see HM. **Services:** El, Ⓔ, ME, CH, ✗, C, BY, SM, SHOM. **Town** Gaz, ⚒, R, Bar, ✉, Ⓑ, ≠, ✈ (Dinard). Ferry: Portsmouth, Poole or Jersey.

DINARD: **HM** ☎ 02·99·46·65·55, Slip, ⚓, M €1.91 (afloat) €1.25 (drying), P, D, L, temp AB; **YC de Dinard** ☎ 02·99·46·14·32, Bar; **Services:** ME, El, Ⓔ, ✗, M, SM. **Town** P, D, ME, El, CH, ⚒, Gaz, R, Bar, ✉, Ⓑ, ≠, ✈. ⊖ 02·99·46·12·42; Ⓗ 02·99·46·18·68.

Extract 13: Port Information – St Peter Port

ST PETER PORT

TIDES −0439 Dover; ML 5·2; Duration 0550; Zone 0 (UT)

NOTE: St Peter Port is a Standard Port, see Tide Tables overleaf.

To find depth of water over the sill into Victoria marina:
1. Look up predicted time and height of HW St Peter Port.
2. Enter table below on the line for height of HW.
3. Extract depth (m) of water for time before/after HW.

Ht (m) of HW St Peter Port	Depth of Water in metres over the Sill (dries 4·2 m)						
	HW	±1hr	±2hrs	±2½hrs	±3hrs	±3½hrs	±4hrs
6·20	2·00	1·85	1·55	1·33	1·10	0·88	0·65
·60	2·40	2·18	1·75	1·43	1·10	0·77	0·45
7·00	2·80	2·52	1·95	1·53	1·10	0·67	0·25
·40	3·20	2·85	2·15	1·63	1·10	0·57	0·05
·80	3·60	3·18	2·35	1·73	1·10	0·47	0·00
8·20	4·00	3·52	2·55	1·83	1·10	0·37	0·00
·60	4·40	3·85	2·75	1·93	1·10	0·28	0·00
9·00	4·80	4·18	2·95	2·03	1·10	0·18	0·00
·40	5·20	4·52	3·15	2·13	1·10	0·08	0·00
·80	5·60	4·85	3·35	2·23	1·10	0·00	0·00

SHELTER Good, especially in Victoria Marina which has a sill 4·2m above CD, with a gauge giving depth over sill. Access approx HW±2½ according to draft; see Table above. R/G tfc lts control ent/exit. Appr via buoyed/lit chan along S side of hbr. Marina boat will direct yachts to waiting pontoon or ❂ pontoons with FW (nos 1-5) N of the waiting pontoon. Pontoons for tenders are each side of marina ent. Local moorings are in centre of hbr, with a secondary fairway N of them. ⚓ prohib. ❂ berths in Queen Elizabeth II and Albert marinas by prior arrangement.

NAVIGATION WPT 49°27'·82N 02°30'·78W, 227°/0·68M to hbr ent. Offlying dangers, big tidal range and strong tidal streams demand careful navigation. Easiest appr from N is via Big Russel between Herm and Sark, passing S of Lower Hds SCM lt buoy. The Little Russel is slightly more direct, but needs care especially in poor visibility; see 9.19.5 and 9.19.9 chartlet. From W and S of Guernsey, give Les Hanois a wide berth. Beware ferries and shipping. Hbr speed limits: 6kn from outer pier heads to line from New Jetty to Castle Cornet; 4kn W of that line.

An **RDF beacon, GY** 304·50kHz, on Castle Bkwtr is synchronised with the co-located horn* to give distance finding. The horn blast begins simultaneously with the 27 sec long dash following the four GY ident signals. Time the number of seconds from the start of the long dash until the horn blast is heard, multiply by 0·18 = your distance in M from the horn; several counts are advised.

LIGHTS AND MARKS Outer ldg lts 220°: Front, Castle bkwtr hd Al WR 10s (vis 187°-007°) Horn 15s*; rear, Belvedere Oc 10s 61m 14M, intens 217°-223°. By day, White patch at Castle Cornet in line 223° with Belvedere Ho (conspic). Inner ldg lts 265°: Front, Oc R 5s; rear, Iso R 2s, vis 260°-270° (10°). This ldg line is for the use of ferries berthing at New Jetty. It extends through moorings in The Pool, so must not be used by yachts which should appr Victoria marina via the buoyed/lit S channel (dashed line). **Traffic Signals** on White Rock (N) pierhead:
● (vis from seaward) = No entry.
● (vis from landward) = No exit (and at New Pier, SW corner). These sigs do not apply to boats, <15m LOA, under power and keeping clear of the fairways.

R/T St Peter Port Marina Ch M 80 (office hrs). Monitor St Peter Port Control VHF Ch 12 (H24) but call Port Control if necessary when within the pilotage area. Water taxi Ch 10 (0800-2359LT). Call St Peter Port Radio CRS Ch 20 for safety traffic. Link calls Ch 62. St Sampson Ch 12 (H24).

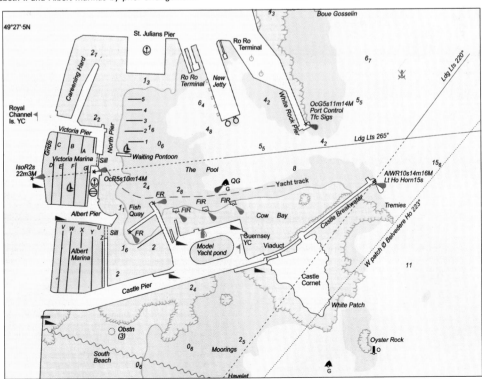

Extracts

Extract 14: Port Information – Granville and Iles Chausey

GRANVILLE

Manche **48°49'·91N 01°35'·97W** ✿✿✿✿✿✿

CHARTS AC 3656, *3659*, 3672; SHOM 7156, 7341; ECM 534, 535; Imray C33B; Stanfords 16, 26

TIDES –0510 Dover; ML 7·1; Duration 0525; Zone –0100

Standard Port ST-MALO

Times				Height (metres)			
High Water		Low Water		MHWS	MHWN	MLWN	MLWS
0100	0800	0300	0800	12·2	9·3	4·2	1·5
1300	2000	1500	2000				
Differences REGNÉVILLE-SUR-MER							
+0010	+0010	+0030	+0020	+0·4	+0·3	+0·2	0·0
GRANVILLE							
+0005	+0005	+0020	+0010	+0·7	+0·5	+0·3	+0·1
CANCALE							
–0002	–0002	+0010	+0010	+0·8	+0·6	+0·3	+0·1

SHELTER Good in the marina, Port de Hérel, 1·5–2·5m. Caution: at ent sharp turn restricts visibility. Access over sill HW –2½ to +3½. Depth over sill shown on lit digital display atop S bkwtr: eg 76=7·6m; 00 = no entry; hard to read in bright sun. The Avant Port (dries) is for commercial/FVs.

NAVIGATION WPT 48°49'·34N 01°37'·09W, 055°/0·95M to S bkwtr lt. Beware rks off Pte du Roc, La Fourchie and Banc de Tombelaine, 1M SSW of Le Loup lt. Appr is rough in strong W winds. Ent/exit under power; speed limit 4kn, 2kn in marina. WCM buoy, VQ (9) 10s Whis, marks Le Videcoq Rk drying 0·8m, 3¼M W of Pte du Roc.

LIGHTS AND MARKS Hbr ent is 0·6M E of Pte du Roc (conspic), Fl (4) 15s 49m 23M, grey tr, R top. No ldg lts, but S bkwtr hd on with TV mast leads 055° to ent. Best appr at night is with Le Loup bearing 085° to avoid pot markers off Pte du Roc; hbr lts are hard to see against town lts. Turn port at bkwtr to cross the sill between R/G piles, Oc R/G 4s. Sill of bathing pool to stbd is marked by 5 R piles, Fl Bu 4s.

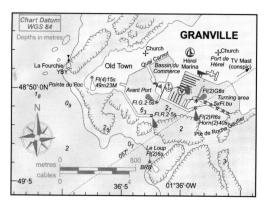

R/T Port VHF Ch 12 16 (HW±1½). Marina Ch 09, H24 in season.

TELEPHONE HM (Port) 02·33·50·17·75; Aff Mar 02·33·91·31·40; CROSS 02·33·52·72·13; SNSM 02·33·61·26·51; ☎ 02·33·50·19·90; Météo 02·33·22·91·77; Auto 08.92.68.08.50; Police 02·33·50·01·00; Dr 02·33·50·00·07; Hosp 02·33·90·74·75; Brit Consul 02.99.46.26.64.

FACILITIES **Hérel Marina** (850+150 visitors) ☎ 02·33·50·20·06, 🖷 02·33·50·17·01, €1·86, ♥ pontoon G (1st to stbd), Slip, P, D, ME, BH (12 ton), C (10 ton), CH, Gaz, R, ⬛, 🍴, Bar, SM, EI, ✕, ⛽; **YC de Granville** ☎ 02·33·50·04·25, 🖷 02·33·50·06·59, L, M, BH, D, P, CH, ⬛, Slip FW, AB, Bar; **Services:** CH, M, ME, EI, Ⓔ, ✕, SHOM, SM. **Town** P, D, ME, 🍴, Gaz, R, Bar, ⬛, Ⓑ, ⇌, ✈ (Dinard), www.granville.cci.fr. Ferry: UK via Jersey or Cherbourg.

ILES CHAUSEY

Manche **48°52'·14N 01°49'·09W** S ent ✿✿✿✿✿✿

CHARTS AC 3656, *3659*; SHOM 7156, 7155, 7161, 7134; ECM 534, 535; Imray C33B; Stanfords 16, 26

TIDES –0500 Dover; ML 7·4; Duration 0530; Zone –0100

Standard Port ST-MALO

Times				Height (metres)			
High Water		Low Water		MHWS	MHWN	MLWN	MLWS
0100	0800	0300	0800	12·2	9·3	4·2	1·5
1300	2000	1500	2000				
Differences ILES CHAUSEY (Grande Ile)							
+0005	+0005	+0015	+0015	+0·8	+0·7	+0·6	+0·4

SHELTER Good except in strong NW or SE winds. Grande Ile is not a French Port of Entry; it is privately owned, but may be visited. Moor fore-and-aft to W 🛟s, free; some dry at sp. Very crowded Sat/Sun in season, especially as drying out in Port Homard (W side of Grande Ile) is actively discouraged. Note the tidal range when ↧ing or picking up 🛟. Tidal streams are not excessive.

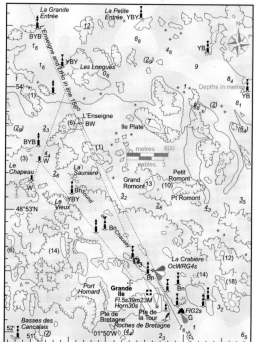

NAVIGATION WPT 48°51'·44N 01°48'·57W, 332°/1·2M to La Crabière lt. The S route into the Sound is easy, via access chan marked by a SHM lt buoy, ECM & WCM bns. The N route requires adequate ht of tide, SHOM 7134 or detailed SDs for transits, and/or local knowledge, but is not too difficult. No access 1/4 to 30/6 to bird sanctuary, all areas E of line from lt ho to L'Enseigne.

LIGHTS AND MARKS Grande Ile lt ho, Fl 5s, is conspic. La Crabière, Oc WRG 4s 5m 9/6M, Y bn; W sector leads into sound; see 9.18.4. By day, La Crabière on with L'Enseigne, W bn tr, B top (19m), leads 332°. From N, L'Enseigne on with Grande Ile lt ho leads 156° to La Grande Entree.

R/T None. TELEPHONE Police 02·33·52·72·02; CROSS 02·33·52·72·13; Auto 08.92.68.08.50; SNSM 02.33.50.28.33.

FACILITIES **Village** FW & 🍴 (limited), Gaz, R, Bar, L, ⬛. Ferry to UK via Granville and Jersey.

Extract 15: Port Information – Diélette

DIÉLETTE

Manche, **49°33´·24N 01°51´·89W** ✹✹⚓⚓☆☆

CHARTS AC *3653*; SHOM 7158, 7133; ECM 528, 1014; Imray C33A; Stanfords 16

TIDES HW –0430 on Dover (UT); ML 5·4m

Standard Port ST-MALO

Times				Height (metres)			
High Water		Low Water		MHWS	MHWN	MLWN	MLWS
0100	0800	0300	0800	12·2	9·3	4·2	1·5
1300	2000	1500	2000				
Differences DIÉLETTE							
+0045	+0035	+0020	+0035	–2·5	–1·9	–0·7	–0·3

SHELTER Good in marina, but some scend near HW when retaining wall covers. Do not attempt entry in strong W'lies. Outer hbr entr dredged to CD +0.5m; accessible for 2.5m draft with Coefficient > 55. W side of outer hbr dries approx 5m (local moorings). Enter marina, about HW±3 for 1·5m draft, over a sill with lifting gate 4m above CD; waiting pontoon outside.

NAVIGATION WPT 49°33'·49N 01°52'·24W, 140°/0·40M to W bkwtr lt. Appr is exposed to W'ly winds/swell. Caution: rky reef dries close NE of appr; cross tide at hbr ent. From/to the S keep seaward of WCM lt buoy off Flamanville power stn.

LIGHTS AND MARKS Power stn chys (72m) are conspic 1·2M to SW. Dir lt 140°, Iso WRG 4s 12m 10/7M, W tr/G top at hd of West bkwtr, vis G070°-135°, W135°-145° (10°), R145°-180°; on same tr is a lower lt, Fl G 4s 6m 2M. Other lts as chartlet.

R/T VHF Ch 09; summer 0800-1300, 1400-2000LT; winter 0900-1200, 1330-1800LT.

TELEPHONE ⊜ 02·33.23.34.02; Aff Mar 02·33.23.36.00; Météo 08·92·68·08·50; CROSS 02·33.52.72.13; SNSM 02·33.04.93.17; YC 02·33·93·10·24.

FACILITIES Marina (370+70 ❂), 02·33.53.68.78, ✆ 02·33.53.68.79; €2.19, D, P, Slip, C (30 ton); Ferry to Cl. **Village**, Bar, R. Also facilities at Flamanville (1·3M).

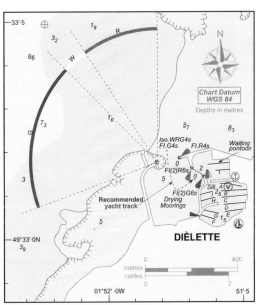

Extracts

Extract 16: Deviation Curve

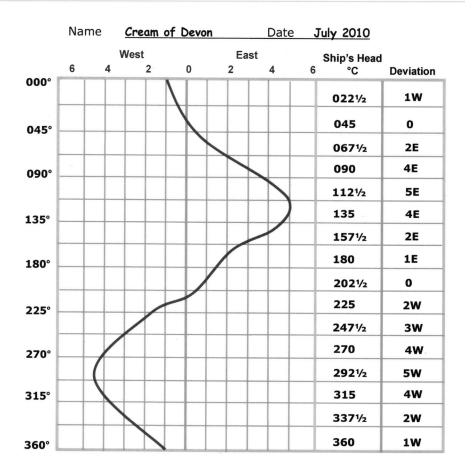

| Name | Cream of Devon | | Date | July 2010 |

Ship's Head °C	Deviation
022½	1W
045	0
067½	2E
090	4E
112½	5E
135	4E
157½	2E
180	1E
202½	0
225	2W
247½	3W
270	4W
292½	5W
315	4W
337½	2W
360	1W

Extract 17: Tidal Differences on Cherbourg–Barfleur

Standard Port CHERBOURG

Times				Height (metres)			
High Water		Low Water		MHWS	MHWN	MLWN	MLWS
0300	1000	0400	1000	6·4	5·0	2·5	1·1
1500	2200	1600	2200				
Differences BARFLEUR							
+0110	+0055	+0052	+0052	+0·1	+0·3	0·0	0·0